FINDING
YOUR
Relationship
FIX

FINDING YOUR

Relationship

FIX

The Four Reasons Couples Seek Counseling

Chris A. Matthews, LMFT

Relationship Counseling Tools, LLC

Finding Your Relationship Fix: The
Four Reasons Couples Seek Counseling

Relationship Counseling Tools, LLC

ISBN (paperback): 9781736921661
eISBN: 9781736921678

Contents

Problems That Develop When Intimate Partners Do Not Feel Safe

- Infidelity
- Financial Issues
- Boundary Intrusions
- Alcohol and Substance Abuse

Barriers That Block Intimate Partners from Feeling Safe

- Lying and Dishonesty
- Violence and Abuse of Power
- Unresolved Trauma
- Sickness and Illness

Problems That Develop When Intimate Partners Do Not Feel Heard

- Communication Issues
- Poor Decision-Making
- Arguments and Fights
- Intimate Disconnections

Barriers That Block Intimate Partners from Feeling Heard

- Defensiveness
- Distractions
- Assumptions
- Judgments

Problems That Develop When Intimate Partners Do Not Feel Understood

- Loneliness
- Lack of Commitment
- Reduction in Relationship Satisfaction
- Parenting Issues

Barriers That Block Intimate Partners from Feeling Understood

- Anonymous Expectations
- Mind Reading
- Blaming
- Emotions

Introduction

Each One Teach One

Each One Teach One, is a phrase that developed during the time of slavery in the United States. Enslaved Africans who learned how to read and write taught their fellow counterparts literacy because they believed it was their responsibility to share what they learned in order to help their companions. Education continues to be a rite of passage for many people living in America and across the world, and I want this book to be a gift to the body of literature surrounding relationships. I became a licensed marriage and family therapist in order to gain specialized training in the art of treating couples and families who strive to better their relationships. Over the course of my journey treating couples, I realized that all of the concerns and issues brought into therapy stemmed from one or both partners not feeling safe, heard, understood, or cared for within the relationship. This book defines the values for each of these four needs and explores the major problems and barriers that are created when these needs are not met. Each section concludes with four basic definitions that summarize the section. I provide several real-life examples and case studies that mirror past clients, and I even provide a few examples from my own marriage. No real names are used in this book and the stories have been altered to protect the identities of the real people. My primary goal for writing this book is to break down the most common issues and concerns clients bring into couples therapy, which stem around the absence of one of the four basic relationship needs to feel safe, heard, understood, and cared for by your intimate partner.

Couples Therapy is the Solution

Couples who enter relationship therapy are met at the door with the understanding that there is only one client being treated—and that is the relationship itself. During my initial meeting with couples, I inform them both that sides will never be taken, because couples counseling is about treating the relationship, not two separate people. The relationship is defined as the space shared by both intimate partners. This approach allows room for each individual partner to be accountable for the individual behaviors they bring into the relationship. Couples counseling is designed to prevent partners from placing blame, because the therapy process extracts accountability for everyone's actions.

This book is not intended to be a "fix-it-yourself" manual, but instead a tool for identifying relationship issues and concerns that can be treated in therapy conducted by a licensed professional who has specialized training in treating couples and families. I have come to realize that, currently in America, relationship counseling is a luxury service that most insurance companies do not cover outright. To date, the majority of insurance companies view couples therapy as an unapproved method for treating and addressing mental health emergencies. My personal experience and work in the field have proven to me that couples therapy is valuable, and my hope is that over time the insurance companies' attitude towards couples therapy will change. But my second goal for writing this book is to provide the public with a clear vantage point for identifying specific issues that can be treated by a well-trained, licensed therapist who has proven experience working with couples using research-based treatment modalities and approaches, and to help couples determine if therapy is a good next step for their relationship.

Chapter 1

REASON ONE: TO FEEL SAFE

When Abraham Maslow developed his "hierarchy of needs," he listed safety as a basic human necessity that follows only behind physiological needs for survival such as water, food, and shelter. Maslow understood that safety impacts all human behaviors and that people make decisions in accordance with how secure they feel. This same theory applies to intimate relationships in that couples make choices based on their level of security with themselves, their partner, and their environment. The decision to engage in sexual intimacy, share financial resources, cohabitate, and start a family are some of the most important relationship choices that are impacted by our feelings of safety and security. In my work conducting thousands of hours of therapy almost entirely with couples, I have found that the desire for one partner to marry or transition the relationship to a higher level is a common concern that motivates couples to seek counseling. In most cases, it is the female partner who begins to ask questions about why their boyfriend has not asked to marry them, and the reason always stems around the male partner's lack of security in either himself, his partner, or the relationship. During therapy, intimate partners are able to process the four basic safety needs—which are financial, physical, emotional, and intellectual—and find ways to move past the barriers that keep their relationship stagnant.

Financial Safety

In today's world, money and financial assets are the most sought-after tools for securing peace of mind and for living our best lives. For most, "living our best lives" can be summed up by having the freedom to make choices without worrying too much about monetary cost. When couples do not feel secure with their current financial status, it directly impacts their level of intimacy—the ability to connect with your partner on a physical, emotional, intellectual, and recreational level.

I often joke with my wife that over our decade of marriage, it felt like my request for sex was granted more often as my earning potential grew. All good jokes have truth behind them, and my hypothesis was confirmed after I read Dr. Harry Fisch's book *The New Naked*, in which he devotes a whole chapter to explaining how financial security equates to couples engaging in more intensified sexual experiences. Usually, after one partner loses a job or the couple experiences some financial threat, their level of intimacy takes a hit, which lends validation to the fact that financial security directly impacts our intimate relationship choices. Therapy assists intimate partners with communicating their feelings surrounding money, so that they can share what their financial needs are in order to feel safe in the relationship. For some partners, this may manifest as a request that their significant other seek a new job that provides a higher income or more time at home. For others, it may be asking for their intimate partner's support as they decide to go to school or seek a training certificate that will give them access to more job choices and career options. I recall a pivotal moment in my own marriage when I asked my wife to support me in starting my own business. She made it clear that I had her support, but she expected me to provide the same quality of life during my entrepreneurial pursuit. I respected her wishes and retained a full-time job until the revenue from the business superseded the income and benefits provided by the job. Having worked with couples from all parts of the world, I learned that in some cultures the male partner has to pay a dowry to the female partner's family before he will be granted her hand in marriage. If the amount does not meet the family's approval, the man will be denied the opportunity to marry because of the lack of long-term security he is able to provide. Money is directly correlated to feelings of safety, and couples leave therapy with a better understanding of how to manage monetary needs that are required to sustain both partners' levels of security.

Physical Safety

It is often quoted that relationships are a fifty-fifty split, but for couples to render the greatest amount of fulfillment, both partners must be willing to put one hundred percent of themselves into the relationship. In order to willingly give all of yourself to another person, you first have to feel physically safe with them. Physical safety can be defined as the ability to interact with your intimate partner without fearing or experiencing any contact that is non-consensual, pain-provoking, discomforting, or that poses a threat to your quality of life.

If you have experienced past abuse or are currently being abused by your intimate partner, you may not have the capacity to open up and give all of yourself to the relationship. Intimate partners who experienced abuse externally from their current relation-ship may still struggle to feel physically safe. If the abuse occurred during childhood or in a past relationship, it has the potential to plague current and future intimate relationships unless it is treated in counseling or with the help of a trained mental health professional. This was evident when I was working with a newlywed couple who sought counseling to process why the female partner shut down when her husband expressed any forms of anger or frustration, even when his emotions were not directed toward his wife. In sessions, we learned that the wife witnessed her father beat her mother throughout the duration of her childhood. As an adult, all forms of aggression provoked a fight-or-flight response in her. She was immediately taken back in time and experienced the same emotions as when she was a child hiding in the closet while her dad beat her mother. This was the first time she connected the dots about how her childhood trauma influenced her current intimate relationship responses. While the couple received marital counseling, the female partner followed my recommendation to seek additional therapy with a trained trauma specialist. This couple was able to use therapy to restore their relationship security by processing how their past traumas were holding them back from feeling physically secure in their marriage.

Emotional Safety

Humans are naturally emotional beings, and we use our feelings as a navigational system to tell us when danger is close, who we should and should not trust, and the best routes to take in order to protect ourselves from getting hurt. A primary issue that couples bring into therapy pertaining to emotional safety involves the pain of infidelity and betrayal. The most common call I receive is from a client seeking couples counseling because they recently learned their partner had an affair, breached their trust, or expressed themselves in a way that scared them.

When we feel surprised by our intimate partner's actions, we experience an emotional reset that turns our lover into a stranger all over again. We question who they are and whether we ever really knew the real person underneath. We ask ourselves if we ever really knew our partner's true motivations, or if perhaps we were speaking with their "representative" all along. These questions are a product of past trauma and can only be answered based on how our partner chooses to proceed in the future. A good future in any relationship is contingent on the hurt partner's ability to preserve enough trust to believe the relationship can be restored. Therapy supports couples with securing emotional safety by helping hurt partners make sense of their pain, assisting with the development of new relationship boundaries, helping partners to constructively express their feelings, and by initiating the process of forgiveness. The therapist does not move faster than the wounded partner and, in some cases, the hurt partner may not be willing to forgive and move forward. Despite the outcome of repair or detachment, therapy gives hurt couples a structured platform they can use to determine what steps are the best for them to take in order to move forward.

Intellectual Safety

Couples often enter therapy because they are not on the same page and feel like their differences in opinions, beliefs, and decisions have begun to pull them apart. But change is inevitable, and even the best relationships experience periods of confusion when partners start to express unbalanced life views, goals, and dreams. We are thinking beings, our minds are constantly changing as we grow, and therapy assists couples with realigning their thoughts so they can feel safe with the direction in which their relation-ship is moving. Knowledge can be the power that drives security or pushes uncertainty, and these uncertainties start to lead couples down a path of not feeling safe. Once we start to crack open the container of intellectual safety, all of our negative thoughts begin to spew out, flooding the relationship with worry, doubt, and confusion. Intimate partners develop an initial baseline of com-fort during the start of the relationship, which is done during the "honeymoon" stage—that special moment towards the beginning of a new relationship when everything feels perfect and it seems like nothing could ever go wrong. Couples then transition through the "storming" phase of establishing norms, and finally settle into their comfort zone during the "performance" stage. When our partner overwhelms us with changes in their professions, hobbies, sexual interests, or fundamental beliefs, this can send our thoughts into overdrive and we relapse back to the storming phase. Our racing thoughts are pulled from places of insecurities and we begin to question ourselves.

This occurred with a couple I was working with who both, at the beginning of their relationship, aspired to be faithful Christians. After they got married, the husband's faith was shaken, and he began to discuss atheism. His wife was so mentally overwhelmed that she went days without being able to talk about his change in beliefs. During this time, she began to question if her husband had fallen out of love with God, and if he was also beginning to fall out of love with her. Her insecurities heightened when she discovered him reading literature describing how Christianity was a dying religion. Their relationship hit a boiling point when he refused to continue to attend church and instead turned toward holistic spiritual practices such as gratitude writing and meditation. They sought out therapy to help define their fundamental differences and, during the process, they were able to find the similarities they continued to share, which assisted them in realigning their marriage. It eventually became obvious that the husband was experiencing a spiritual malnourishment from ingesting the same mundane religious routines and practices. He was on a quest for more and not less. Therapy slowed their thoughts down so they could process their core beliefs and values, which they both found rooted in biblical principles. During one session together, we outlined their moral standards and found they both desired to treat people with kindness, cherish their minds and bodies, take care of their family and community, and demonstrate love and respect towards each other. Over the course of therapy, they took the time to listen and learn how the other one thought, which in turn restored their intellectual safety and marital connection.

The Four Types of Safety Needs for Intimate Partners

Financial: Defining the amount of money and financial assets required for both intimate partners to feel secure in knowing their basic needs, wants, and desires will be met in the present and future.

Physical: The ability to interact with your intimate partner without fearing or experiencing any contact that is nonconsensual, pain-provoking, discomforting, or that poses a threat to your quality of life.

Emotional: Feeling as if your partner has your best interests in mind at all times, based on verbal and nonverbal communication that sup-ports your individuality and ability to safely explore the world.

Intellectual: Operating on the same life course as your partner, defined by sharing coexisting world views and goals associated with family, spirituality, finances, physical wellbeing, and social belief systems.

Problems that Develop When Intimate Partners Do Not Feel Safe

There are several problems that can develop between couples when one or both partners do not feel safe. The four major problems couples routinely bring into therapy are issues stemming from infidelity, money, relationship boundaries, and substance use. These problems tend to correlate with underlying issues that stem from each partner's history, and issues tend to crop up during times of relationship distress. I will introduce each of these problems and how intimate partners receive assistance with treating them in couples therapy.

- Infidelity
- Financial Issues
- Boundary Intrusions
- Alcohol and Substance Abuse

Infidelity

Infidelity is defined as any action that threatens or breaches the intimate relationship contract with regard to how both partners choose to conduct themselves around other people outside of the intimate relationship. The problem I witness through my lens as a therapist is that the majority of couples entering counseling have failed to write down or make clear what their relationship guide-lines are. I share with couples that when they purchase a car or home, it's necessary to draw up paperwork outlining the standards for a loan. Establishing an intimate relationship should be no different than entering any other formal contractual agreement. Developing an agreement of standards, clearly outlining the needs of both parties, safeguards both parties from misunderstandings. Intimate partners can protect themselves from future misunderstandings by properly communicating and documenting what they expect. Each partner is responsible for communicating their own unique perspectives around what they believe counts as infidelity. Moreover, each partner needs to have the freedom to update or make changes to the agreement based on future relationship experiences. For example, if two heterosexual intimate partners consent to having opposite sex friendships at the initiation of the relation-ship, this standard may change if one partner is caught engaging in an act that threatens the binding relationship agreement. This could be one of the partners choosing to send inappropriate text messages or social media correspondences to an opposite-sex friend. When the other intimate partner reads the exchange, they may ask that the relationship agreement exclude the ability to sustain opposite-sex friendships until their trust is restored. They may even go so far as to view the act as grounds for terminating the entire intimate relationship altogether.

Choosing to be with a specific intimate partner is always a choice, and people need to choose wisely. Once that choice is made, the next step is to design an agreement that lists a set of standards that protects each other's investment of time. When I share this in sessions with some couples, they question if developing a relation-ship contract will distort their romance or natural flow. My reply is that accountability does not eradicate spontaneity or creativity. Instead, ensuring security increases the possibility of more spontaneity, because it provides a playing field for both partners to feel safe. In order for intimate partners to feel safe and prevent the onset of infidelity, they have to establish agreed-upon rules that define how they expect each other to conduct themselves with others outside of the intimate relationship.

Common Types of Infidelity

The two types of infidelity are *emotional* cheating and *physical* cheating. Affairs are the combination of emotional and/or physical cheating that occur over multiple interactions with the same per-son or several outside partners. All forms of infidelity are rooted in the act of breaching intimate relationship standards of physical and emotional conduct, defined by the betrayed partner. The betrayed partner is the individual who experiences sorrow, anger, and distress, often followed by grief, after learning their partner broke the intimate relationship circle of trust.

Since every person is different, some partners find it harder to forgive certain acts of infidelity over others. In my work with couples who bring issues of infidelity into therapy, affairs are always the hardest to treat because both partners are simultaneously experiencing grief and loss. The offending partner or cheater is coping with not having their needs met in their primary intimate relationship. The betrayed partner is dealing with having security in their relationship stripped away after learning they have been sharing their partner with another person. Although the thought might be that the cheating partner is at fault and doesn't deserve any sympathy, since they're the ones who initiated the betrayal, a good couples therapist understands that both partners are dealing with loss and problems with the relationship. To support the work that has to be done in therapy, I always suggest that each partner speak to their primary care doctor or a psychiatrist to find out about how medications might assist in coping with their emotions. This is highly recommended when either partner's ability to function is threatened for an extended period of time.

Rebuilding an intimate relationship after infidelity is difficult work, and couples should start the process expecting to feel an insurmountable level of emotional pain. In order for couples to rebuild, they have to process what happened and why it happened. This can manifest itself as the betrayed partner wanting to know every detail of the affair, and if the cheating partner fails to be descriptive or leaves out information, trust will never begin to be reestablished. The greatest satisfaction I receive from doing couples therapy comes from working with partners who are able to rebuild a better relationship after infidelity. These couples are some of the most resilient human beings I have ever met, and it is always an honor to be a part of their healing and rebuilding process. At the onset of therapy, I inform couples dealing with infidelity that they will never get the same relationship back, but that they can choose to build a stronger, better relationship. I use the metaphor of a house fire—the original home has burned down, and no matter what they do, it will not come back. Hurt partners never forget that the infidelity happened, but they can choose to rebuild their relationship on the same lot. Not all is lost, because couples can sift through the ashes of their old relationship, find aspects that still work, and take them into their new union.

I recall working with a couple who, before and after the infidelity, did a great job co-parenting, sharing household responsibilities, and providing financially for each other and their family. These characteristics were not only transferred into the new relationship, but served as the motivation they both needed to success-fully do the hard work required to rebuild a stronger relationship after infidelity.

Why Therapy Helps

It does not matter if a man or a woman cheats because they are both making a choice to betray their intimate partner and the relation-ship. There is no reason that justifies infidelity, because the choice to leave or reassess the relationship prior to cheating is always an option, which makes the unfaithful act of cheating a selfish choice. Partners who cheat should never be treated or made to feel less than human. If given the opportunity by their betrayed partner to rebuild the intimate relationship, they have to be willing to submit to what is required for healing to take place. The first stage of infidelity treatment requires the cheating partner to relinquish all privacy at the discretion of the betrayed partner. With one couple I treated, the male partner was an avid marathon runner who told his wife he was at a race when he was actually away for the weekend having sex with his mistress. She requested he no longer run out-of-town races unless she was present. In this case, the cheating partner understood his actions produced a result that required him to give up something he deeply enjoyed, but that was the cost he was willing to pay in order to rebuild his marriage. His wife further requested he no longer have a cell phone or access to their joint debit or credit cards, since he used money out of the family account to fund the romantic getaway with his infidelity partner. As his wife regained her trust in him and felt safe again, he was able to regain these freedoms, but it took a lot of hard work on his part. His wife also accepted that she had to work on herself. Her work started with a willingness to gain a better understanding of what led her husband to seek another intimate partner outside of the marriage. For the first time since they got married, she provided him with the space in therapy to express his dislikes and desires. Despite her pain, she was able to receive what was said and apply the information from therapy to become the wife he desired and needed. They both became better listeners and overall communicators, which facilitated the healing process. Their process was ever changing over the nine months of couples therapy, but they kept fighting. They did encounter a set-back at the beginning, when the male partner made contact with the infidelity partner and failed to tell his wife. They endured feelings of belittlement as the male partner left for work each morning without a cell phone and with an empty wallet. Through all of the treatment stages they both kept fighting to get better as individuals and intimate partners. Their work paid off and at the conclusion of therapy they had a new and improved marriage equipped to handle the adversities of life. I will never forget that, in the initial call with the wife, she asked me if I could salvage their marriage after infidelity. I replied, "No"; but if they both chose to put the work in and not give up, I could help them build a new and improved marriage. They both did the work, and what they accomplished in therapy not only rebuilt their marriage, it preserved their family of five. I never met the children, but I believe the work done in therapy was just as important for them as it was for their parents.

The Four Primary Types of Infidelity

1. *Cheating:* Engaging in any form of emotional or physical contact with another person live or via technology that your intimate relationship partner may deem as inappropriate, hurtful, or disrespectful based on the agreed-upon relationship standards you both defined.

2. *Affair*: Allocating resources such as money, time, and attention toward sustaining a secretive physical and/or emotional secondary intimate relationship designed to fill a void that is not currently being met by your primary intimate partner.

3. *Exploring*: Operating in any manner that appears to be an attempt to establish a secretive romantic connection with another person outside of your intimate relationship.

4. *Engaging:* Sustained contact with any person with whom your intimate partner has requested you end all communication because your involvement with that person makes them feel unsafe.

Financial Issues

Couples will often blame their finances for the reason they sought out therapy—however, the *mismanagement* of finances and money is usually the real reason or problem. Couples who seek therapy to process or heal from pain associated with lies stemming from money are treating a barrier that prohibits safety (this is discussed in more detail later on in this chapter, where I address lying and dishonesty). Financial problems are connected to feelings of safety and security, because money is a basic need that influences daily living—and when this need is threatened, people begin to operate from a place of desperation and fear.

Take for example the husband who loses his job but gets up and leaves the house every morning as if he is reporting to work, because he fears that when his wife finds out she will leave him. Other examples include the wife who attempts to cope with her shopping addiction by taking on a second job to pay off store credit cards, because she fears her husband will leave her if he learns she is a compulsive shopper. Not all financial issues stem from a lack of money or wealth—some partners are unable to disassociate past traumas induced by poverty as a reason for their money issues. These partners may have a problem spending money, which in turn forces them and their family to go without their basic needs being met, despite having the monetary means to meet all their needs and wants. Some intimate partners choose to use money as a measuring tool to define their lives, instead of a vehicle used to explore and travel through life.

How Therapy Helps

Therapy aids intimate partners with processing cognitive and emotional attitudes pertaining to money, so they can safely make joint financial decisions that benefit them both. I tell couples that the establishment of a marriage or committed long-term intimate relationship is similar to two large companies deciding to merge their finances. The merger of finances can take place in a variety of ways, and therapy helps couples develop a system with which both partners feel safe. They can choose to manage the financial books together, which usually involves one partner operating as the chief financial officer who regulates spending and bill pay. Couples can opt to have separate finances and take turns paying specific bills they both mutually accrue, such as utilities, groceries, and vacations. Some couples choose to sustain private accounts and have a joint account they equally contribute to that covers shared expenses such as lodging, childcare, daily essentials, and other items they use in tandem. I find that couples who have a greater sense of mutual trust for one another also find it easier to develop a system that makes them both feel secure when it comes to money management. When I explore my own marriage, my wife and I have opted to combine all of our money because of the simple fact that, based on our marriage license in our state and without a prenuptial agreement, both of our finances are seen as joint anyway. We also operate in conjunction with our strengths and align our monetary decisions with the values we established at the beginning of the marriage. We both made a choice to value the pursuit of life experiences such as vacations, attending con-certs, and being able to provide our kids with extra resources such as summer camps and tutoring. We value these experiences over the desire to own expensive possessions. Our alignment in values provides us both with the security of knowing the other person will not come home with a brand-new sports car or an expensive item we didn't mutually agree upon. For my own therapy practice, couples who are seeking financial planning are referred to colleagues in my network who specialize in budgeting, retirement, and overall money management. The couples I treat use therapy to dive more deeply into exploring their monetary belief systems and values. One partner may desire to make more money so they can spend more money, and the other partner may desire to spend less money so they can save more money. In therapy, couples learn how to better communicate so they can communicate their ideas and beliefs around money in a way that their partner can understand. Overall, therapy helps intimate partners with aligning their financial beliefs and values, so they will be better equipped to work with a financial planner who can assist them in developing and meeting their monetary goals.

The Four Financial Values and Beliefs Treated in Therapy

1. *Earning:* The ability for both intimate partners to produce the desired or agreed-upon amount of income in order to sustain individual, relationship, and family needs and wants.
2. *Debt:* The production of accrued financial resistance that can limit the attainment of wealth and financial freedom when it outnumbers liquidity and assets.
3. *Spending:* The disbursement of cash, credit, or assets in order to receive something in exchange that is perceived to be of equal or greater value.
4. *Saving:* The preservation of money in order to consolidate an accumulation of wealth and security, or to accomplish specific financial goals.

Boundary Intrusions

Boundaries are identifiable markers used to regulate emotional safety and relationship security. Some examples of boundaries that couples use include notifications, mutual agreements, and plans.

These tools help intimate partners with managing external influences like family, friends, work, and hobbies so they do not become a wedge that creates conflict between the couple. Early in my own marriage, my wife would act displeased with me when I came into the house while on the phone. She requested that we establish a mutual agreement not to enter the house on the phone, because she felt like I should first greet her with a hug and kiss when coming through the door. Moving forward, I completed all my calls in the garage before entering the house, and respected the boundary we developed to ensure she does not feel ignored when we reunite after going a whole day apart. Establishing boundaries in our relationship originated during our courtship phase. I expressed to her that I felt ignored when I'd call her and she wouldn't answer the phone, even if she was on the other line. I asked her if she would be willing to make me the most important person in her life in exchange for me doing the same for her. The result of this conversation was that we agreed to get off the other line and respond to each other's calls immediately. In the event we are on a business call or speaking to someone we haven't spoken to in a while, we click over or send a text message to inform each other we received the call and plan on calling back once we're finished. I find that, during therapy, partners will complain that they did not know when their partner was coming home, and when they attempted to reach them by phone the call was ignored. When a partner refuses to pick up the phone or overlooks the planned time they said they would be home, a relationship boundary is crossed. Couples also credit relationships with family members, friends, and coworkers as another common form of boundary intrusion. For example, one partner might be unable to successfully manage an overbearing parent who attempts to gain decision-making power over how the couple manages their intimate relationship, children, or professional careers. Another example is the friend who feels the never-ending urge to provide critiques about your partner in an effort to convince you to end the relationship. Outside of close family and friends, I have also witnessed couples bring issues into therapy surrounding religious groups, clubs, and other organizations that have operated as a form of boundary intrusion. In one extreme case, an intimate partner joined a cult like organization that challenged his marital vows by persuading him to view the members of the group as more important than his wife. Boundary intruders can also come in the form of activities and behaviors that threaten the relationship. I have heard partners in therapy share that they feel like it is a losing battle to convince their significant other to spend time with them because of their partner's desire to watch sports or their obsessions with reality television shows. Some people report feeling like they come in second or third place behind their partner's employment, kids, or leisure activities. An intimate partner's desire to feel special can sometimes need to be renegotiated.

Why Therapy Helps

Therapists assist couples with establishing, communicating, and restructuring boundary lines so each partner can sustain a high level of security in knowing they are the most important person in their partners' lives. When working with couples, it is common to sense the tension right away when one partner feels they are treated secondary to a job. In problematic cases, work boundaries were never established, or they did not get updated as the couple experienced changes in their employment. This was the case for a couple who sought out therapy because the female partner started to feel like her boyfriend progressively began to place his career before her. During the onset of the relationship, he worked as a local truck driver. After two years in his role as a commercial driver, he desired to make more income, and that led him to start his own trucking company. The startup of a new business produced a greater demand on his time, and he began to falter on their original agreement. The boundaries that were eventually set by way of a mutual agreement involved both partners only working on weekdays, which allowed them to spend their weekends together uninterrupted.

As the business grew, the male partner encountered instability with drivers and unexpected labor issues that required more of his time and attention on the weekends. The female partner noticed the agreed-upon line between work and time together being crossed, and she was starting to feel left out. Through therapy, the couple enhanced their communication and ability to realign their boundaries. This looked like the male partner inviting his girlfriend to ride along with him so they could sustain an intimate connection while he worked. The couple arrived at this conclusion in therapy by processing each other's feelings, needs, wants, and expectations. Prior to therapy, the male partner failed to include his girlfriend in the business because he feared she would not be supportive of his dream. He later learned that his girlfriend desired their weekends to include his work because her only concern was that they have time together, even if that involved having to do work with the business alongside him. The female partner learned to enjoy sup-porting the business, because it produced more uninterrupted time to have deeper conversations while she rode in the truck with her boyfriend. She eventually quit her job after retaining a commercial driver's license herself, so they could do team driving and take on larger contracts that required longer trips and more quality time together. The business awarded them both more financial freedom and brought them closer to reaching their future marital and family goals.

Not all couples experience this level of compatibility when it comes to setting boundaries, and in some cases one or both partners may have to work harder in therapy to identify the boundary intrusions before they can be restored. This was evident for a couple I met with, where the male partner felt like his wife placed her career above him and the kids. During the initial phase of treatment, he identified multiple examples that included his wife choosing to come home late because she worked extra hours at the office. The breaking point that led the couple into therapy was when the wife failed to be mentally present during the family's weeklong vacation because she could not stop responding to emails and phone calls. In therapy, we identified that the wife worked so hard at her job because it awarded her the security she did not have as a child. This revelation came about in couples therapy with her husband present, while she processed her childhood experiences between her own mother and father. She recalled how her father discarded the family to run off and start a new household with his mistress. She went into detail expressing how that event in her life was pivotal for developing her relentless work ethic, driven by the fear of being abandoned again. I helped her to see that in her efforts not to feel hurt again, she was becoming her father and choosing her work over her family in the same way he chose his mistress over his family. After a moment of silence, she turned to her husband and embraced him while weeping uncontrollable tears and murmuring apologetic sentiments. Therapy provided her with the break-through she needed to see work as a threat to her family, because it was blocking her from being a present wife and mother. The couple was then able to reestablish boundaries that involved the female partner not continuing to make decisions that placed work ahead of spending quality time with the family. Work is a popular boundary intruder because we rely on our jobs for financial stability and, in some cases, our jobs define a large part of our identities, which makes it easy to get lost in our professions.

Other common intimate relationship boundary intruders include parents, siblings, and close friends. These members of our network have oftentimes known us longer than our intimate partner, and they tend to adopt a sense of entitlement when it comes to inserting their thoughts and opinions about our lives. One topic that couples learn to protect and keep sacred during couples counseling is their relationship with each other. When we share detailed information with our family regarding fights, negative feelings, or how our intimate partner wronged us, we are choosing to distort the future perspectives our loved ones will have toward our partner. Before my wife and I were married, I recall sharing private information about my then-girlfriend with my mother—and sure enough my mom used what I had told her as ammunition to paint my wife in a negative light after we became pregnant with our first child unexpectedly. This event completely destroyed what little trust that had been built between my mom and wife during our dating phase and worse, made my wife totally uncomfortable around her. It took years to restore what was lost, and I had to build a wall between the two of them in order to regain my wife's trust back. It is easy to fall into the trap of oversharing relationship information with family and friends, and therapy helps intimate partners with setting guidelines for information dissemination so both intimate partners remain secure.

The Four Primary Types of Intimate Relationship Boundary Intrusions

1. *Family*: Nuclear or secondary family members who attempt to gain or impose their own decision-making power, influence, or unsolicited advice onto one or both intimate relationship partners.

2.   *Friends:* Nonfamilial, close relationships that are perceived by one partner to be more influential or import-ant than the intimate relationship.

3.   *Employment:* A position designed to acquire revenue that has the potential to become more valuable than the people it is intended to support.

4.   *Leisure:* Hobbies, activities, or external organizations that can reduce relationship quality when one partner begins to feel like they are competing for their partner's attention and time.

Alcohol and Substance Use

I started my clinical career treating addiction as a substance abuse counselor, while I worked toward retaining the education and training needed to become a couples therapist. I still maintain my credentials as a licensed clinical addiction specialist, because alcoholism and drug abuse are the most common co-occurring disorders that many couples bring into therapy along with their other issues. Typically, one or both partners will share their accounts of a really heated argument that led them into therapy, and I will ask if either partner was consuming alcohol or other substances at the time. Without failure, more often than not, the couple will con-fess that one or both of them were drinking wine, beer, or liquor, but will immediately strike down the belief alcohol played a role in the dispute. In movies and on television, alcohol consumption is constantly marketed as a party starter, but while working as a therapist, I commonly hear couples describe how the overconsumption of alcohol incited a fight or other type of relationship dispute. This is because alcohol and other drugs limit inhibitions and influence people to say and do things they normally would not say or do when they are sober. After attitudes have become readjusted and tempers calm down, couples will blame their substance use for why they raised their voices, cursed at each other, or in extreme cases became violent. The problem with this forgetful behavior is that the emotional scars and bruises do not dry up with the alcohol. Couples will find themselves in a constant spiral of drinking to have fun, then overconsuming, fighting, retreating, coming back together, and then repeating the same cycle week after week, month after month, and year after year. This emotional carousel only stops when one or both partners become completely sober or one partner chooses to end the relationship because of a substance-induced event that was unrepairable.

Not all substance use solicits aggressive responses, and some couples bring concerns into therapy pertaining to how their partner's consumption of alcohol or drugs makes them distant. People use drugs to feel what they desire, and that could be the craving for more energy, to calm down, or to have an extrasensory experience. I tell people that if drugs did not work, no one would use them, but they create problems when the user begins to get used by the drug. The attachment a user develops with a drug begins to mirror a domestically violent relationship. The user starts to get beat up physically, mentally, and emotionally by the drug, but still cannot find the strength to stop using. Just like the intimate partner who keeps going back or refuses to leave the abusive relationship, drug users find themselves trapped by fear, self-doubt, or low self-worth, which keeps them using the substance.

Outside of the use of legally prescribed medications that are properly managed under the care of a physician, which requires routine follow-up visits, drug use should be prohibited because our minds, bodies, and lives are constantly changing. The major dis-advantage of self-medicating with illicit drugs is the absence of a trained professional to regulate and manage the changes in dos-ages and side effects. This can lead to overdoses, addiction, and withdrawals, which in some cases can be lethal depending on the substance being abused. Alcohol and drugs by themselves are not a problem—the issues come when users begin to display signs and symptoms of substance abuse, withdrawal, or intoxication defined by the Diagnostic and Statistical Manual of Mental Disorders (DSM), the international manual that all mental health providers use to diagnose both substance abuse and mental health disorders. The DSM lists eleven signs and symptoms that are associated with diagnosing clients with mid, moderate, and severe substance use disorders. Clinicians look for these signs and symptoms when conducting comprehensive assessments, which include administering screenings, questionnaires, and bio-social clinical interviews. Other factors, such as family and health histories, occupation, legal issues, and personality traits also should be considered when determining if one can safely decide to engage in substance use or should remain sober.

Why Therapy Helps

Alcohol consumers and drug users are known to be very defensive when approached in any manner that challenges or threatens their continued use. When working with couples who self-report substance use, the first step is to establish a rapport to assist with lowering their defenses. This approach is phase one of a therapeutic method called "motivational interviewing." Motivational interviewing is essentially a conversation that assists with provoking change. In couples therapy, this exchange is usually directed toward one partner who has displayed multiple signs and symptoms of having a substance use disorder. This therapeutic process is helpful in getting the substance-using partner to make changes by identifying how their alcohol or drug use has negatively impacted themselves, their intimate partner, and family. It takes time to implement this process, and the end goal is to get the sub-stance-using partner or the couple ready to seek substance abuse treatment. The length of time for getting clients ready to enter treatment varies.

I experienced working with a couple that took twenty sessions over a five-month period before the male partner was ready to seek treatment for his addiction to alcohol. Couples therapy helped these two intimate partners strengthen several areas of their relationship, but the male partner's alcohol consumption continued to unravel their progress, setting them back to square one. Each time he chose to go on a drunken rampage, drown his sorrows in an eighteen pack of beer, or leave his wife alone to manage the kids for an entire weekend, he pressed the reset button. His wife chose to ride his emotional roller coaster, driven by the false belief that one day he would learn how to manage his alcohol consumption on his own. The couple's turbulent, alcohol-induced ride came to a stop when the female partner used therapy to identify and accept her role in creating the problem. She was unaware that her methods of attempting to help her husband by protecting him from the negative consequences actually fueled his alcoholism. Once she realized alcoholism was a disease that could only be treated with sobriety, she stopped enabling his drinking. As a result, her husband lost his job and hit rock bottom. Treatment became the only solution, because seeking help for his addiction was the only way he could prevent losing his wife and kids. While the male partner enrolled in an intensive outpatient treatment program, the couple continued joint therapy and identified that they both came from backgrounds that contained alcoholic parents. The male partner's drinking behaviors modeled his father and the female partner's enabling behaviors mimicked her mother. Ultimately, they both came to terms with the fact that their behaviors aligned with a genetic blueprint and they had become their parents. This light-bulb moment was pieced together during the residual work they did in couples therapy. The male partner successfully completed a substance abuse treatment program and began to actively participate in Alcoholics Anonymous in order to keep his addiction in remission. The female partner joined a support group at her church, which assisted family members of alcoholics. She used the group to further process her needs and learned how to support her husband's recovery efforts. Overall, therapy operated as the driving force this couple needed to save and repair their marriage and family.

The Four Intimate Relationship Losses Caused by Alcohol and Drug Use

1. *Loss of Control:* The substance-using partner's good decision-making power, which allows them to regulate their alcohol and drug use, is negated.
2. *Loss of Trust:* The substance-using partner begins to lie about or underreport their alcohol or substance use to avoid arguments or requests from their intimate part-ner to stop them from using.
3. *Loss of Existence:* The substance-using partner feels a need or desire to engage in the use of alcohol or drugs all the time, just to feel present or to escape life.
4. *Loss of Safety:* The substance-using partner becomes physically or verbally aggressive, irritable, or undesirable to be around when under the influence or withdrawing from alcohol and drugs.

Barriers That Block Intimate Partners from Feeling Safe

Couples who exhibit behaviors or concerns that pose as barriers often bring problems into therapy associated with not feeling safe. These barriers are individual issues that block intimate partners from feeling safe. This continues to fuel relationship problems, and the couple will never start to heal until the barriers are removed. The four most common barriers that cause relationship problems related to partners feeling unsafe are lying and dishonesty, violence and the abuse of power, unresolved traumas, and sickness and illness.

- Lying and Dishonesty
- Violence and Abuse of Power
- Unresolved Trauma
- Sickness and Illness

Lying and Dishonesty

One of the perks that comes with establishing an intimate relationship is the ability to feel free to be yourself. This freedom is based on the foundational belief that your partner accepts the past and present you. Lying or being lied to by your intimate partner contradicts this relationship principle and, in turn, prevents you and your partner from feeling safe in the relationship. This concept is applied mutually to both partners—the partner telling the lie and the partner receiving the lie. When working with couples where one partner cheats, lying is usually a common side effect that delays the treatment process. When the cheating partner lies, they are attempting to control how their hurt partner feels, but this always backfires when the hurt partner finds out the truth.

The hurt partner will lie about their forgiveness progress and will attempt to convince themselves and their partner they have moved past the infidelity. The hurt partner's lie usually comes out when they are no longer able to conceal their triggers, flashbacks, or insecure feelings, which means they still need more time to heal from the infidelity. Their lie damages the relationship because the cheating partner no longer trusts that their repenting actions will ever be enough. It is necessary for both the hurt partner and the cheating partner to be honest in order to regain connection. Honesty is similar to credit—it takes a long time to acquire, and even longer to repair. Infidelity and betrayals are like bankruptcies and should be expected to take a while to heal. However, during the healing process, if done with truth and honesty every step of the way, the couple will rebuild a stronger relationship than before.

Other reasons intimate partners lie are fear, lack of respect, and habit. Humans are designed to self-preserve, and that includes steering away from anything that could cause pain or discomfort. The old saying "the truth hurts" is real, because when we tell our partners the truth, we risk hurting them—and, in turn, hurting ourselves. The truth is still the best option because it prevents deceit, which is a deeper level of betrayal that can negate all the good experiences that took place after the original lie was told. When an intimate partner learns they were lied to, the first thing they ask is for a time stamp to determine how long the lie was told. The lied-to partner then processes the time period between when the lie was told and when they learned the truth. That time between the lie and the truth is questioned for authenticity. When working with one couple, the male partner kept secret that he had cheated on his wife for five years. When she learned about the affair from a mutual friend, she felt like those years were also a lie too. She questioned if her husband had been connecting with his affair partner over the past five years every time she was not in his presence. That included every private phone call, email, and business trip. The pain she experienced from the truth was too much for her, and she decided not to work toward restoring their marriage. Couples lie primarily out of fear, but the longer the truth is concealed, the greater the amount of deceit.

Why Therapy Helps

Couples therapy helps with dishonesty by holding each partner accountable for their words and actions. The therapist is the unbiased third-party recorder who documents what is said in the therapy sessions and matches the couple's words with their actions. When I was treating a couple that was attempting to heal from infidelity, the male partner expressed that he desired to rebuild a monogamous relationship with his girlfriend. I then proceeded to hold both partners accountable by requesting they outline and sign a monogamy agreement which described the behaviors they expected from each other, in order to sustain their committed relationship. Both partners also defined the actions they would take if the agreement was broken. Two weeks later, the male partner was caught making sexual advances toward other women, and his actions went against the contract developed in therapy. The female partner called me when she found out to thank me for the work we did in therapy and to share that she was no longer in need of my help. She further elaborated that, by attending therapy, she had become empowered to set boundaries on her boyfriend's unfaithful actions, which led her to terminate their intimate relationship. The only treatment for dishonesty in couples therapy is accountability. If one or both partners are unable to be accountable for their own actions, then at that point I make the referral for individual therapy. Couples therapists treat the relationship or the space between the two intimate partners, not two individuals. If one or both partners choose not to control themselves and their continued actions lead to an unsafe relationship, then at that point couples therapy is no longer the best form of treatment.

The Four Types of Lying and Dishonesty

1. ***Omission***: Deliberately withholding information (pertaining to people, places, events, and actions) from your intimate partner in an effort to avoid consequences, emotional arousal, and unintended pain or harm.
2. ***Protection***: Making a choice to mislead or recreate a narrative in order to safeguard your partner which, in turn, does more harm than good after the intimate partner learns that aspects of the relationship were built on untruths.
3. ***Control***: Using falsehoods as leverage in order to sustain an authoritarian position in the relationship or fulfill a self-esteem deficiency.
4. ***Perception:*** The inability to comprehend why and how lying to your partner can result in the intimate relationship reaching a point where it can no longer be salvaged or repaired.

Violence and Abuse of Power

There is never an excuse or reason that is acceptable for intimate partners to be violent or abusive toward each other, period. Violent acts consist of any engagements between intimate partners that causes either person physical, mental, or emotional harm. Abusive behaviors are actions designed to control or hurt your partner by using manipulation, intimidation, threats, isolation, withholding resources, or gatekeeping relationships with children, pets, and family members. It is not uncommon to learn that abusive partners have an untreated history of being abused themselves or displayed patterns of abuse in previous relationships. Identifying signs of violence and abuse early in the relationship is key to protecting yourself. Partners who develop the belief they can change the abuser or think their abusive partner will get better usually end up enduring the most pain, or sometimes even death. This is why it is imperative to dissolve the relationship immediately before transitioning to living together, having kids, or intertwining your life with an abusive partner. Most abusive or violent partners gradually display signs of their negative behaviors but attempt to conceal their actions through a false sense of love and care. To protect yourself from these forms of manipulation it is important to work on yourself prior to engaging in an intimate relationship. People who do the work of building up their self-esteem through accomplishing life goals, establishing their finances, developing their ideal body composition, and evolving strong and healthy friendships prior to pursuing a relationship are less likely to attach to or stay in an abusive intimate relationship.

Why Therapy Helps

Based on the American Mental Health Counselors Association (AMHCA) code of ethics, "the primary responsibility of mental health counselors is to respect client autonomy, dignity, and pro-mote client welfare." Counselors are trained to promote and protect clients' welfare by establishing and sustaining a safe place to conduct therapy. If one or both partners are actively engaging in violent behaviors toward the other, couples counseling is not recommended until the violence has ceased. The research on con-ducting couples counseling with clients who are actively engaging in Intimate Partner Violence (IPV) is extremely limited. Based on a systemic review and meta-analysis that consist of comprehensive literature searches of 1,733 citations. Only six studies investigated the effectiveness of couples counseling as a viable treatment method for treating relationship violence. Per my graduate-level training, I recommend that clients seek individual therapy if they are in a current relationship that is physically violent. With the referral to seek individual counseling, I am respecting the client's autonomy while promoting their welfare in hopes they will be empowered in individual therapy to make healthier and safer relationship choices. Choosing to treat partners together who are actively engaging in violent behaviors toward one another is unsafe for the couple and the therapist.

Safety was a major concern with one couple with whom I was initiating treatment—they became violent outside in the parking lot prior to coming in for their first therapy session. I heard yelling and screaming outside, and I ran over to the window to see what was going on. To my surprise, the couple fighting in the parking lot were the people with whom I was scheduled to conduct therapy. The office complex I was practicing therapy out of employed onsite security, who intervened by separating the couple and calling the police. I followed up with both partners the next day and recommended that they seek individual therapy. I informed them they did not meet the criteria for couples therapy because it was not safe. The female partner agreed with my assessment and followed through with my referral to start individual therapy. She also signed a release and exchange of information form, enabling me and her individual therapist to have two-way communication. The male partner turned down my recommendation and did not seek out individual therapy. I later found out that this couple routinely engaged in physical altercations, but did not report these events when I conducted my phone screening prior to their initial session. I also learned that the male partner threatened the female partner's life on several occasions and her attempt to get them both into couples therapy escalated the violence even more. Upon following up with the female partner, she chose to dissolve the relationship because of the work she completed in individual therapy. My belief is that if I had ignored the violence and attempted to treat this couple together in counseling motivated by the thought *I can fix them,* then the female partner may be dead today. Couples therapy does not fix or break up partners who are violent and abusive. Violent and abusive partners have to work on fixing them-selves before they can fix their relationship, and that work is done through completing intervention programs and individual therapy.

The Four Barriers to Dissolving an Abusive Intimate Relationship

1. ***Fear***: A state of anxiousness or hyper arousal from the anticipation of your intimate partner inflicting life-altering or life-ending pain.

2. ***Chaos:*** Learning to cope with a violent intimate relationship by numbing yourself through the use of alcohol and drugs, or engaging in other self-harming behaviors.

3. ***Distorted Thinking:*** Feeling like you deserve the abuse, believing you caused the abuse, or thinking you can stop or change the abuser.

4. ***Captivity:*** Feeling trapped and imprisoned by an abusive intimate partner due to the fear of losing your children, citizenship, or access to basic needs such as money, shelter, or employment if you decide to leave the relationship.

Unresolved Trauma

When we choose to establish an intimate relationship, we are choosing to grow with our partner's past, current, and future experiences. One or both partners may bring past or current traumas into the relationship. If trauma has not been processed or managed properly, usually in therapy, then it can result in one or both partners not feeling safe in the relationship. Trauma is defined by the American Psychological Association as "an emotional response to a terrible event like an accident, rape, or natural disaster." Trauma is subjective to the person's reaction to an experience, so we cannot assume just because our partner had or witnessed a horrific experience that they are going to respond with trauma-based symptoms. The onset of trauma symptoms can also be delayed or can manifest later if induced by physical or psycho-logical triggers. The intensity level of the traumatic experiences can vary based on factors such as age at the time of the experience, direct life impact, and resiliency and coping skills. Intimate relationships can feature single-trauma couples (where one partner is a trauma survivor) or dual-trauma couples (in which both partners have a history of trauma). In single-trauma couples, the partner dealing with trauma symptoms may shut down, exhibit mood swings, or withdraw from their partner, creating the potential for a confusing and unsafe relationship. In dual-trauma couples, both partners may initially be attracted to one another by their shared ability to understand each other's pain, but also may experience more intense or volatile exchanges.

Trauma has the potential to create an environment where safety for one or both partners is an issue. For example, a client of mine named Julie was a rape survivor who just had a four-month-old infant and was fearful to place her daughter in a childcare center. Julie's husband Mark was upset because they were constantly fighting over the best daytime care options for their daughter, so Julie could return to work. Julie was fearful that her daughter would be mistreated, because Julie was raped by her uncle who watched her while her mother was at work. Mark was afraid Julie would decide not to return to work so she could stay home with their daughter. This troubled Mark because he feared having to get a third job in order to provide for his family in the event Julie decided not to go back to work. Although past trauma is at the root of Julie and Mark's current childcare issue, it is common for couples to misdiagnose trauma issues as independent communication problems. Indeed, at the surface of the issue, the couple is not properly communicating their individual needs. However, the root of the issue is much deeper than simple communication differences—and therapy helps identify the feelings and emotions that drive our decisions, which in turns helps us communicate better.

Why Therapy Helps

Well-trained therapists take their time peeling off their client's layers of thoughts, beliefs, and emotions in order to find out what is underneath the original problem or complaint that is brought into therapy. This process first starts by gaining the client's trust through establishing a rapport. Once a relationship is formed, the clinician can then develop a therapeutic alliance with the couple. The alliance is the steering wheel that allows the therapist to stimulate the clients' sharing of thoughts, memories, and feelings from past experiences. When this process is in full effect, the therapist is then able to identify past traumas that drive the emotions sup-porting the problematic actions and behaviors. The therapist high-lights "inflection points" from the stories told by the client that have been overlooked or suppressed. Inflection points are isolated traumatic events or experiences that have altered the clients' feelings and distorted their behaviors. During couples therapy, both partners simultaneously go on an exploratory journey together, identifying past traumatic events that provide reasoning for the current problematic behaviors. The therapist is the tour guide leading the couple back in time as they gain a better understanding of how their issues originated. As this process unfolds, intimate partners have the opportunity to display empathy and support for each other. The connection that is strengthened in couples therapy helps the intimate partners instill more patience and understanding as they find solutions to issues that trigger their past traumas.

Julie and Mark, the couple mentioned earlier, were able to find a childcare option that worked. This happened when Julie opened up in couples therapy about her fears stemming from her own experience as a rape survivor. Julie's sharing led Mark to be more patient and to offer solutions that supported Julie feeling safer about their daughter being placed in a childcare facility. Mark identified childcare centers that offered live surveillance that fed video right to Julie's phone, so she could view the baby whenever she felt triggered or experienced a flashback. He also suggested that the baby start off in childcare part time and then progress to full time when Julie became more relaxed with the baby in another person's care. Therapy further assisted this couple in how they moved for-ward with all of their challenging joint-parenting decisions. Julie gained more comfort expressing herself with regard to how her past experiences influenced her current decision-making process. Mark continued to display patience when he observed Julie's dis-comfort, instead of becoming frustrated with Julie and shutting down like he had in the past. The therapy room gives couples who have experienced traumatic events a safe place to process their stories, display empathy for one another, and develop emotionally safer ways of moving forward in their relationship together.

The Four Signs of Trauma that Negatively Impact Intimate Relationships

1. ***Flashbacks:*** A dream or mental visualization that stems from a past trauma and produces negative emotional stimuli such as anxiety, sadness, fear, or anger.
2. ***Triggers:*** Actions, words, or events that unknowingly prompt flashbacks or other trauma-related signs and symptoms in one or both intimate partners.
3. ***Isolation:*** The desire to separate from an intimate partner who has not experienced trauma, because of their lack of empathy or understanding.
4. ***Division:*** The erosion of connectivity, communication, and positive experiences caused by unprocessed trauma symptoms such as flashbacks, triggers, and isolation.

Sickness and Illness

During the course of an intimate relationship, it is not uncommon for one or both partners to become ill. When sickness arises, the ailing partner's hope is that their intimate partner will take care of them. Unfortunately, not all couples have the resources to manage sickness and, as a result, the sickness can evolve from being a physical illness into mental distress and illness. The toll physical illness takes on a relationship can cause a couple to experience chronic stress and emotional fatigue. The brunt of this emotional fatigue usually falls upon the caretaker partner and tends to be more prevalent in couples managing a long-term illness. Caretaker partners can become overwhelmed by the constant demands of providing support, and forget to take care of themselves. They might gradually begin to engage in poor dietary and sleep habits, reduce their social activities, and may feel guilty when they are not doing activities that support their sick intimate partners. Over time, they too can break down and no longer have the physical and emotional energy required to care for their partners or themselves.

This was the case for a couple I treated, who initiated therapy because the wife was failing to take care of herself while supporting her sick husband—and, as a result, infidelity occurred. She became her husband's primary caretaker after he was diagnosed with multiple sclerosis. At the onset of the disease, the husband had to stop working and the female partner transitioned into the role of sole provider and primary caretaker for their family of two. After a full year of treatment, the husband was able to regain employment and function independently. Despite his recovery and reinstatement of independence, he still depended on his wife to take care of him. His wife began to feel taken for granted and, when she attempted to express how she felt, her husband played the victim instead of taking the time to listen. To escalate matters, prior to the husband's diagnosis, the couple experienced a plentiful and fulfilling sex life which had since become nonexistent. The multiple sclerosis impeded the husband's ability to perform sexually, making it challenging for the couple to engage in the same sex life they had previously enjoyed. The female partner understood how this impacted her husband's self-esteem, but still expressed a desire for him to explore other ways to provide her sexual pleasure and connection. His refusal to put forth an effort to increase his ability to take care of himself, his lack of determination to explore new ways of pleasing his wife sexually, and his choosing to ignore his wife's feelings created a fertile ground for infidelity. Although I believe there is no excuse for an intimate partner to cheat, we can't ignore the fact that certain factors make it easier for one partner to justify seeking intimacy outside of the committed relationship. In this case, the female partner felt like cheating on her husband was the only way she could get her needs and wants met, since he had given up on having a sex life. Unfortunately, like the majority of cheating partners I counsel, she later found out that infidelity always takes away more than what it gives. When her husband learned that she lied about an out-of-town work trip, and instead attended a sex-filled getaway in the wilderness with a coworker, he contemplated ending twenty years of marriage. The positive light in which he viewed his wife was extinguished by her betrayal.

Why Therapy Helps

Talk therapy does more for the spirit and mind than the body, but it does aid couples who have lost direction due to the onset of sickness. Therapy helps couples by providing a safe place to have hard con-versations that are directed by a professional who is trained to man-age the emotions in the room. These in-session dialogs are saturated with thoughts, feelings, and emotions stemming from how the illness has impacted the relationship. Oftentimes, the caretaker partner loses their voice or doesn't feel invited to share what they need or want to feel happy in the relationship. The focus shifts to the sick partner, which allows the caretaker partner's needs to fall by the wayside.

If this goes unchecked over a sustained period of time, the caretaker partner can become burned out. Burnout shows itself in several different forms and develops at different rates for all people. Some partners have the potential to care for each other during sickness without missing a beat, while others break down after a few weeks unless they take breaks or lean on additional supports. In the couple we discussed earlier, the female partner finally came up for air three years into her husband's sickness and realized she had gained fifty pounds, hadn't taken a vacation, and had developed resentment toward the man she was taking care of. This made it easier for her to believe she was entitled to cheat on her husband. Therapy allocates the space for the caretaking partner and the partner battling sickness to both share how the management of the illness has taken a toll on the relationship. The sick partner may too also harness negative emotions that they developed during the treatment process. If the ill partner feels a lack of support, empathy, or understanding, then they may start resenting their caretaking partner. This is to be expected in cases where the ill partner believes they are not receiving the same level of care they provided in an instance where the roles were swapped, and they had been the caretaker. Once the couple sheds light on how they feel and what they need while in therapy, they can mitigate their negative feelings. It is our negative thoughts, beliefs, experiences, and feelings that get in the way of us sharing what we need and expect from our ill partner or caretaking partner. Therapy gives couples a vessel in which to pour their emotions, before they bubble over and further disrupt the relationship.

The Four Barriers of Sickness and Illness

1. *Resources:* The money, time, access to care, and human capital required to treat a serious illness.
2. *Treatment:* A plan or regimen of care including the examinations, surgeries, rehab, and medications required to properly treat acute and chronic physical and mental health issues.
3. *Planning:* The process of preparing for sickness or illness by securing access to insurance, education, preventative care, and a social support system in case either partner is affected by a health crisis.
4. *Coping:* The ability to process and continue daily functioning that supports the sustainment of a healthy inti-mate relationship while treating or managing the signs and symptoms associated with acute and chronic physical and mental health illnesses.

Chapter 2

REASON TWO: TO FEEL HEARD

Listening and speaking are the two most important roles inti-mate partners share in their relationship. The giving and receiving of verbal and nonverbal communication pro-vide both partners with the opportunity to teach each other how they feel, how they think, and most importantly, how they desire to be treated. The golden rule is to treat people the way *you want to be treated*, but I tell my clients to practice the platinum rule, which is to treat their intimate partner the way *they desire to be treated*. In order to follow this platinum rule, couples have to properly send and receive verbal and nonverbal messages back and forth.

Equally important is your partner's ability to articulate words in a manner that pull you toward them and make it easier to listen when they are speaking. Intimate partners make it easier for themselves to be heard when they remember not to oversaturate their messages with long tangents of information. Partners who slow down and allow each other time to process the message being sent tend to feel heard more often. Another common error made by speakers is saying the same thing over and over. Speakers may think this practice of repetition helps their partner better hear them, but instead this technique frustrates the listener and makes them less likely to engage in the conversation. Speakers should deliver their messages with intention, and listeners need to be mindful of creating the space for their partner's messages to be effectively received. Listeners and speakers must first work to create the best environment in order to sustain engagement and guarantee hearing is taking place. This starts by checking to ensure you and your partner have both tended to individual physiological needs prior to beginning a dialogue. Satisfying hunger, using the restroom, and scheduling the conversation after getting some rest all provide partners the best chance of engaging in active listening. Once listeners have prepared their bodies to hear their partner, they then must equip their minds to be present.

Focusing on your intimate partner's words, tone of voice, and body language as they speak help you decode the messages they are sending. To do this effectively requires that you avoid simply waiting for your turn to speak, and instead becoming an empathic listener. Empathic listening is challenging because it forces the hearing partner to block out their own thoughts, feelings, and beliefs for the moment, and make space to solely receive what the speaking partner is saying. Couples usually struggle with this outside of therapy, because they believe listening to messages from their partner automatically equates to consenting or agreeing with what is being said. I constantly debunk this myth in therapy and educate intimate partners on the fact that empathic listening does not force your partner's beliefs upon you. Instead, it simply allows them to share without being interrupted, judged, or cut off, which are all behaviors that make speakers not feel heard by their intimate partners. Listening and speaking are the foundations of feeling heard, and when partners fail to hear, four major relationship problems are created. Couples that do not feel heard will bring problems into therapy stemming from communication, decision-making, arguments, and issues sustaining intimate connections.

The Four Actions that Allow Your
Intimate Partner to Feel Heard

1. ***Active Listening:*** The process of asking your intimate partner open-ended questions in order to affirm, reflect, and summarize what they are saying and feeling.

2. ***Emotional Identification:*** The utilization of empathic listening in order to allow your partner to share their unique perspective as their truth, while remaining nonjudgmental and seeking to find the emotions they are communicating.

3. ***Perspective-Taking:*** Choosing to step outside of your own thoughts, beliefs, and viewpoints in order to experience how your intimate partner sees the world.

4. ***Responsiveness:*** Acknowledging that you heard what your partner said by responding with verbal and nonverbal cues of validation and questioning in order to learn more in the event that the message was not fully received or comprehended.

Problems that Develop When Intimate Partners Do Not Feel Heard

When intimate partners fail to hear each other, they are not able to accurately transmit messages back and forth. Communication problems will soon follow when partners experience difficulties sending and receiving messages. Communication issues will induce complications with decision-making, and soon couples will find themselves in an environment that supports unresolved arguments. Endless arguments will develop into heated fights that break down intimate connection. When partners do not feel heard, they will suffer from issues that stem from their inability to communicate, make joint decisions, resolve arguments, and sustain intimate connections.

In this chapter, we'll discuss the four main problems that stem from partners not feeling heard:

- Communication Issues
- Poor Decision-Making
- Arguments and Fights
- Intimate Disconnections

Communication Issues

Without healthy and effective communication, it is impossible for partners to hear each other. This creates major relationship problems. To explore how intimate partners can develop communication issues when they are not heard, I am going to use the five axioms of communication as a template. The five axioms of communication were developed by Dr. Watzlawick and are influenced by the work of Dr. Bateson, Dr. Bavelas, and Dr. Jackson, who are pioneers within the marriage and family therapy community. These four theorists are known for their research around how couples and families communicate and interact within their family systems.

Axiom One: Intimate partners cannot *not* communicate. It is impossible to not communicate, just as it is impossible not to make a choice. This is because choosing nothing is still a choice— and saying nothing still communicates a message to your intimate partner. When one or both partners choose not to engage verbally or physically, they are still sending messages to each other. The messages may be *I am not interested, I am upset,* or *something is wrong, and I want you to fix it or find out why I am not talking to you.* Often times, couples will contact me to schedule therapy, and will claim the problem is that they do not communicate. These couple are communicating, they just may not have good communication practices, or their styles of communication may not be aligned, so they cannot not communicate.

Why Therapy Helps

Therapy helps by assisting partners with regulating their emotions so they can effectively send and receive messages. When intimate partners get hurt and become angry, they may revert back to their communication blueprints, which can manifest as the infamous silent treatment. The problem with not speaking to your partner is that they are then forced to guess what you are thinking and feeling. This behavior also leads your partner down the unguided path of attempting to respond to your feelings without first hearing what you desire. Instead of setting your partner up for failure, therapy helps by teaching couples how to properly take space. Properly taking space from your partner so you can both discuss the problem or issue later is a three-step process. The first step is sharing with your partner that you are upset and need some time or space apart prior to engaging with them. The second step is to inform your partner on how long you anticipate the separation will last and where you'll be if you choose to leave the home. The final step is the most important and results in the partner initiating the taking of space, keeping their commitment, and seeking out the offending partner after the designated space period has concluded. This process prevents the hurt partner from applying the silent treatment. It further gives both partners time to regulate their emotions and prepare for the healing process or reconciliation to take place. Taking space also prevents the accused partner from feeling anxious or guessing when they will have the opportunity to repair their wrongdoing. Taking space is a process that requires practice, and very few couples master these steps on their first few attempts.

Axiom Two: Intimate partners communicate using the content and relationship. The content within communication is the topic or subject that is being discussed, and the relation-ship is how both partners interpret or conceptualize the content. Intimate partners communicate on the relationship level when they express the content through the filters of the following assertions: *"How I see myself,"* *"How I see you,"* and *"How I see you seeing me."* An example of all three of these relationship assertions in action may look like a female partner who becomes upset at her boyfriend for forgetting to call her after he gets off work. She begins her communication by speaking to him in an accusatory tone as she inquires about his day. Still ruminating over the missed phone call earlier, she begins to question her physical attractiveness, which is how she sees herself. Next, she leads into questioning her boy-friend's commitment because she views the females he works with as more attractive than her. This leads her to further consider her boyfriend's willingness to initiate an outside relationship. She then constructs a narrative in her head that her boyfriend did not call her after work because he is no longer physically attracted to her. She allows her thoughts to snowball and she is now convinced he sees her as someone who is naive. In the middle of the conversation she asks her boyfriend if he thinks she is stupid because she knows he is cheating on her with a coworker.

In this example the female partner viewed herself as unattractive, her boyfriend as unfaithful, and accused him of seeing her as stupid. The content originated from the missed phone call, but when cycled through the girlfriend's relationship assertions, she communicated with an accusatory and attacking tone. The girlfriend's communication stirred up conflict because her boyfriend instantly became defensive when he was accused of cheating. The female partner was unable to comprehend her own metacommunication. Metacommunication is the message behind the message—this is better understood as the decoding of what is being communicated in addition to the words being used.

Why Therapy Helps

Couples that seek therapy to improve their communicate learn how to send the messages they intend their intimate partner to receive. In the example above, the female partner intended to send a message that communicated her feelings of insecurity. Instead, she allowed her own assertions to override the content which was based on the fact that her boyfriend broke his normal pattern of calling her when he got off work. Therapy helps couples find the underlying feelings and communicate them directly. From therapy, the girlfriend would learn how to identify the emotion she is feeling and how to communicate it clearly so she can be heard by her boyfriend. This could be as simple as her saying, "I noticed that you did not call me like you usually do when you got off work. This made me feel a little insecure because you work with a lot of beautiful women and my last boyfriend cheated on me with one of his female coworkers." This would allow her boyfriend the space to learn more about why his girlfriend is hypersensitive to his change in routine. It also gives him the opportunity to reassure his girlfriend of his commitment to her. If partners lack the self-esteem, self-value, or self-worth required to communicate on this level of vulnerability, then I will refer them to seek individual therapy in conjunction with couples therapy. Individual therapy helps partners independently establish confidence in themselves so they can be vulnerable with their intimate partner. Vulnerability is required to communicate on a deeper level, but is risky for partners who have not healed from past relationship hurts. Being vulnerable requires courage because when it is present, partners open themselves up to being hurt. The vulnerable partner can feel misunderstood in the event that their partner is unable to properly decode or acknowledge the message being communicated. When this process takes place in couples therapy, the clinician can operate as a crutch that supports understanding. With practice, couples are able to learn how to identify each other's emotions quicker. Over time, partners will gain the ability to read each other's meta-communication and hear the feelings behind the words being said.

Axiom Three: Intimate partners establish communication sequences based on stimuli and responses. Intimate partners create different communication sequences based on how they interpret their partner's actions as a response or stimulus. For example, a couple may develop a sequential communication pat-tern that starts by decoding an act as a response (for example, "I don't initiate sex as often because you have not proposed and there-fore have not demonstrated a commitment level that makes me feel secure"), whereas the other partner may decode the response as a stimulus (for example, "I have not proposed because I can't see myself marrying someone who doesn't want to initiate sex that often"). This communication axiom illustrates the dilemma that intimate partners find themselves in when they rely on their partner's actions to determine their own behavior.

Why Therapy Helps

Intimate partners who come into therapy with ultimatums usually find themselves at a relationship impasse. An impasse is a block-age or standoff that is produced because the couple is unable to effectively communicate what they need or want. Partners continue to spin their wheels and establish communication sequences that feel like they are taking a ride on a merry-go-round. In the example above, the couple was following the lead of the other, but they failed to communicate an agreed-upon starting point. Therapy provides couples with clarity so they can map out a direction that moves the relationship forward. The therapist shines a light on what each partner wants so they can develop a plan of action that meets both of their individual needs. The partner that desires more commitment would be instructed to communicate the value they feel marriage would provide to the relationship. They may share that they believe marriage offers a veil of protection in the event they become pregnant. Their portrayal of marriage is centered around a need for security. Safety is the key that would unlock their desire to initiate and engage in more sex. The partner who wants sex may communicate feeling undesired or not wanted. When asked by the clinician to explore their beliefs, they may share how they feel unattractive because in previous relation-ships they never had to initiate sex. After both partners share their perspectives in therapy, they are now more informed and can use the new information to work on dissolving the impasse. With their newfound knowledge regarding each other's thoughts and feelings, they can develop alternative communication sequences that bring them closer to getting their relationship needs met. Therapy helps intimate partners establish new communication sequences that are used to break through impasses.

Axiom Four: Intimate partners communicate digitally and analogically. Digital communication refers to the "what" or the actual words being used, and analogical communication refers to the "how" or nonverbal cues that are transmitted by intimate partners. Communication issues arise when partners send digital and analogical messages that do not align. It is all too common for one partner to ask if something is wrong and receive the reply, "No, I am fine." The partner inquiring didn't just ask the question without first identifying some type of analogical code first, which indicated that something might be wrong. Even if the other partner was truly fine, in order to prevent future issues, it is necessary to address the reason behind the analogical communication or the troubling nonverbal expression. That could look like saying, "I am fine—I am just wondering if we turned the alarm on before leaving the house." This response validates that there is not a problem in the relationship. Intimate relationships produce a sensitivity that instinctively makes each partner question first if they are the problem in the event they observe something is wrong.

Why Therapy Helps

Intimate partners who have been dating or have sustained a committed relationship for a long period of time develop the habit of relying on their instincts. The problem with instincts is that they pull from the most relevant information we have about our partner. Our instincts will fail us in times of relationship turmoil if we do not constantly work on getting to know our intimate partner better every day. This is because our partner is forever changing, and if we stop receiving updates on their growth, our data will become obsolete.

Staying updated with your partner requires making time for daily engagements. Therapy holds partners accountable by emphasizing the need for them to make time to spend together. This can happen through the assignment of experiential homework that requires partners to go on dates, engage in meaningful conversations, and perform heartfelt gestures, which all work in concert to jump-start the intimate relationship. When couples deliberately spend time together, getting to know each other better, they will also create opportunities to update their digital and analogical communication. A partner learned that his wife has developed a craving for a new restaurant in town while sharing about her workday. He received this update by observing the pleasurable expression on her face and the uptick in her vocal tone as she described how good the food tasted. A few weeks later he makes reservations for them to have dinner at the same restaurant. He instinctually made a choice to take her to that specific restaurant because of the update he received while spending time engaging in daily conversation. Therapy enhances couples' digital and analogical communication by helping them remember the importance of spending quality time together.

Axiom Five: Intimate partners engage in communication roles that are symmetrical or complementary, which are both influenced by power and control. Symmetric communication occurs between intimate partners who share equal degrees of power and influence. Couples that practice symmetrical communication have similar beliefs and values. These couples can be balanced and function as a unit if both partners demonstrate positive characteristics such as a belief in teamwork, mutual respect, and gratitude. Partners who engage in symmetrical forms of communication do not always work well together if they both are domineering and exhibit the same negative traits that lead to problematic communication styles. Negative or unhealthy couples that engage in symmetrical communication styles will bump heads if both of them refuse to change. Positive couples that utilize symmetrical communication have a better chance of growing together and developing healthy communication patterns when they share an equal balance of power and control. Complementary communication happens when couples act in roles that accommodate each other. This can look like one partner taking on an authoritarian or parental role, and the other partner accommodating by operating in a childlike role. If this is done by choice it can be a good style of communication that makes the relationship run smoothly. If the structured partner communicates by giving the unstructured partner a "honey to-do" list, similar to how a kid is given a list of chores, and neither partner has an issue with this, then this form of complementary communication may work for that couple. Complementary styles of communication are problematic when the power differential is distributed by force and not by choice.

This was the case for a couple I treated where the female partner gave her husband a spending allowance because she made more money. He felt like he was being treated like a child, but the female partner felt justified in her form of complementary communication because she didn't feel like her husband was financially responsible. In therapy, she shared that her husband had a history of spending the money he needed to pay bills on entertainment and eating out. After he failed to pay the electric and gas bills, she refused to allow him access to managing the finances moving forward. Communication issues arise when partners are not in alliance with their roles or desire to be in a different role that is influenced by power and control.

Why Therapy Helps

Each partner brings into the intimate relationship an array of their own unique positive and negative characteristics. Couples use therapy to help identify the habits and behaviors that have the potential to benefit or hurt the relationship. The therapist is not emotionally invested, which makes it easier for them to highlight each partner's strengths and weaknesses. During therapy, partners learn how to use complementary and symmetrical communication to validate and deescalate conflict before it even starts. This hap-pens by identifying the feelings that drive their partner's decisions.

With the couple mentioned earlier, the therapist would help them first discover the emotions they experience and then help them both communicate the feelings to each other. The female partner who is better at paying bills on time states that she values security and peace of mind. The male partner who likes to spend money expresses that he seeks to have the freedom to surprise and excite his partner because he enjoys showing her a good time. After the couple find out what the other values, they can then speak to complement that need or want. This could be achieved by the female partner asking the male partner if he would like to have the freedom to use the money left over after the bills are paid to plan their entertainment for the month. She also validates that she desires her partner to show her a good time, but finds more enjoyment from the entertainment experiences when they do not compete with their basic needs being met. He, in return, expresses appreciation for her organizational skills and shares how he also finds more pleasure in knowing they can have fun without jeopardizing basic necessities. The couple shifted from a complementary to a symmetrical style of communication because there was a realignment of power. From therapy, both partners gained the ability to get their needs met and learned how to transition their communication from complementary to symmetrical after they felt like a balance in power was reestablished.

The Four Tools Used by Intimate Partners to Communicate

1. *Verbal Messages:* The transmission between intimate partners of spoken words or auditory signals used to communicate directives, questions, thoughts, feelings, and emotions.
2. *Nonverbal Messages:* The display or demonstration of messages that do not use words but still communicate emotions, thoughts, and feelings—intentionally or unintentionally.
3. *Transmitter:* The partner who is in the role of speaker or whose turn it is within the conversation to send a verbal or nonverbal message in order to have a need met, initiate engagement, or respond to a request.
4. *Receiver:* The partner who is attempting to hear and decode the verbal or nonverbal messages that are transmitted so they can proceed with rendering validation, feedback, or a request to better understand the message that was originally sent.

Poor Decision-Making

Intimate partners develop power differentials based on their roles and responsibilities within the relationship. When one or both partners do not feel heard, they are unable to responsibly regulate roles and power bases, which influence how decisions are made in the relationship. The partner who feels like their voice does not count will typically also be the partner who feels like they have less power. Over time, the unheard partner will seek to find room to be heard by any means necessary. This can manifest as making decisions solely based on the need to balance power, even if their actions are done at the cost of taking value away from the intimate relationship. There are five different basic types of power that influence how relationship decisions are made between intimate partners. I will explore each of these types of powers and share how therapy helps partners make decisions based on their operation within each power system.

Types of Power that Influence Decision-Making in Intimate Relationships

Coercive: The use of this type of power is unsafe in intimate relationships because it does not provide both partners with a mutual benefit or gain. Coercive power requires that one partner be punished if they do not obey the command or meet the wishes of the other partner. The command is usually something that one partner would not have willfully consented to without the threat of harm or danger coming by way of the requesting partner.

An example of this power in use might be if one partner threatened to contact the Immigration and Customs Enforcement office if their illegal alien partner decided to end or dissolve the intimate relationship. This type of power is also commonly known as extortion and blackmail. Couples who deploy coercive power tactics strip away trust because they are putting each other in positions of oppression. Although it is usually one partner in the relationship who will use money, influence, children, or status as a way to establish coercive power, couples who share equal positions can use this form of power on each other. In therapy, I see this happen when couples decided to dissolve their intimate relationship and are fighting for leverage to hurt each other. Independently, coercive power is used in abusive relationships where one partner is at the mercy of the other due to money, citizenship, or other controlling factors.

Why Therapy Helps

If couples are attempting to dissolve their relationship or if one partner is ambivalent about staying in the marriage, they may find benefit from discernment counseling. Discernment counseling helps couples see the relationship for what it is, rather than for how they would like it to be. This form of counseling has the potential to prevent the use of coercive power because couples can use the process to brace for the possible impact of the relationship's end. Discernment counseling concludes with one of three outcomes for the couple: the couple remains in the relationship as is, separates or divorces, or makes an attempt at reconciling the relationship through long-term therapy. Coercive power is more likely to be used in abusive relationships and when partners feel angry or con-fused about the direction of the relationship. During the process of discernment counseling the therapist helps couples find a sense of direction and offers guidance on how to proceed with the relationship. In the event coercive power is being used toward one partner, the therapist will highlight that as abuse. If the controlling partner chooses to continue the abuse then a referral will be made for them to seek individual therapy. Therapists can only report abuse to the authorities in the event that it involves a minor, elderly individual, or a member of the special needs population. Domestic abuse and domestic violence are not reportable offenses because two consenting adults have complete autonomy to leave or stay in the relationship. I would be remiss if I failed to mention that not all relationships are this simple, where one partner can simply leave if they feel unsafe or threatened. However, there is little a couple's therapist can do outside of making the proper referrals.

Reward: Reward power is when a positive stimulus is exchanged for the fulfillment of a need or want being met by a partner. Couples use reward power when one partner offers to provide something that only they can provide, as an incentive to get something they want. An example of the use of reward power is when one partner requests that the other cleans the garage in exchange for a home-cooked meal. The power is rooted in exclusivity, because the partner exchanging the meal for the deed may be a great cook who chooses not to prepare food that often. Reward power is another form of compromise that allows partners to get their individual needs met in a tit for tat fashion. *You do this for me, and I will do this for you.* When the reward is seen to be of equal or greater value than the request, partners usually get the outcome they are seeking.

Why Therapy Helps

Some couples enter therapy dizzy from going around in a circle of argument loops that fail to end with solutions with which both partners agree. I hear couples say that they will keep having the same never-ending fight about an action they desire from their partner that never gets consistently done. A partner may ask their significant other to fold laundry, wash dishes, or clean the bathroom, but the request eventually falls to the wayside after a few days of inconsistent action. Therapy helps partners use their reward power as a form of "pull motivation" in order to build the habits they desire from each other. Pull motivation attracts your partner to the action, and over time creates a behavioral change that develops into a habit. The therapist does this by helping the couple experiment with the implementation of different stimuli that renders a sustained result.

I recall one partner who wanted her husband to wake up with her at least two mornings per week so they could talk while she got ready for work. This was a challenging request for him to sustain, because he did not really have to wake up for work for another two hours after she left for work. It was later discovered that he desired his wife to initiate more opportunities for them to have sex. Using the information both partners presented, they devised a plan in therapy that entailed the female partner initiating sex each night her husband chose to wake up with her that morning. The use of reward power helped both partners consistently get what they wanted. The female partner stated that she had developed a deeper connection with her husband because he was choosing to wake up several mornings per week to talk while she got ready for work. This made it easy for her to keep her end of the bargain and initiate sex on the nights following the mornings he woke up with her and engaged verbally while she prepared for work. From this experiential homework assignment, the couple tapped into their use of reward power to consistently get what they both wanted.

Expert: Expert power originates when one partner has a greater skill or knowledge base in an area compared to the other. When one partner feels they are better suited to make a decision, complete a certain task, or regulate a joint responsibility, then they will implement their expert power to persuade the other to allow them to do so. This may manifest itself as one partner soliciting to be solely in charge of cooking the family dinners because they took a course that specialized in healthy meal preparation. The partner seeking the dinner responsibilities will argue points stemming from having a greater knowledge or skill base to complete the task. Couples develop problems with the implementation of expert power when partners lose confidence in each other's perceived knowledge or skill set. When this happens, couples will need to have discussions stemming from the renegotiation of roles and responsibilities. Feelings and egos have the potential to be hurt, which makes this process problematic. If the partner who has been responsible for cooking dinner is told that the food does not taste good, then their expert power is threatened.

Why Therapy Helps

Couples often enter therapy with preexisting wounds that developed after learning their intimate partner is displeased or unsatisfied with them. These ego-shattering moments create hardship because one partner learned for the first time that their significant other did not view them as skilled or knowledgeable in an area, and instead had proclaimed themselves to be an expert. When an intimate partner has their expert power threatened, they can divert to becoming distant or unattached in the relationship. Therapy helps mend the hurt caused by this phenomenon by giving couples a platform in which to learn how to satisfy each other.

The therapist may start by dissociating the displeasure experienced from the identity of the partner who feels hurt after their expert power is criticized. This process entails prompting the displeased party to illustrate other areas and ways their partner satisfies them and adds value to the relationship. Once the hurt partner reestablishes confidence that their significant other is content in several other areas of the relationship, they will then be more receptive to learning how they can improve at the task in question. The therapist will control the pace of the dialogue to ensure both partners remain safe enough to express their true feelings pertaining to the why and how. For one couple I was working with, the why for a female partner who expressed a displeasure with her husband's sexual performance related to his inability to be creative. The how was associated with the instructions she gave her husband during therapy which assisted him with the information he need to please her sexually. Therapy helps by rebuilding the hurt partner's ego so they can learn how to become the expert their significant other desires. This process happens during counseling when couples humble themselves and become each other's students. When we allow our partner to teach us what they like, we gain the expert power needed to keep them satisfied in the relationship.

Referent: Referent power is special for couples because it is enforced by the respect intimate partners have for one another. Referent power is activated when couples are influenced to make decisions based on the admiration they have for each other's personality, beliefs, and values. An example of referent power at play might be a husband choosing to incorporate more vegetables and fruits into his diet because he admires his wife's commitment to a healthy life-style. Intimate partners use their referent power to lead each other by the examples they provide. When our loved one is influenced to follow our lead because of the respect and admiration they have for us, referent power is at play. Referent power is hard to gain but can easily be lost. If the wife in this example stops eating healthfully, she risks disabling her referent power. Her husband may view her lack of discipline as a weakness, causing a distortion in how he once saw his wife as someone whom he admired for her self-control.

Why Therapy Helps

Couples who experience dramatic changes in their relationship—such as one partner losing a job or becoming ill—seek therapy to help manage these adversities because they impact the pendulum swing of referent power. When the partner who was historically seen as the defined breadwinner or financial provider is no longer able to work, they risk losing respect. Respect is built on esteem, confidence, and outcomes, which makes it ever changing.

Ideally, we would expect our partner to support us when we experience difficulties, but this is not always the case. Some couples rely on the help of a therapist to assist them with redefining roles and responsibilities, so their relationship can regain balance. In therapy, couples are able to identify alternative traits in each other that influence admiration and respect. The partner who was injured and placed out of work can reclaim their self-respect by keeping a positive attitude instead of adopting a victim mentality. Although the partner is temporarily unable to provide the same level of monetary value, they can replace the money by exemplifying the determination to regroup so they can return back to work. Their partner will then be inclined to gain even more respect for them because of the grit they displayed during times of adversity. Therapists help couples regain referent power by providing intimate partners with opportunities to find alternative ways to demonstrate tasks that earn back respect, admiration, approval, and loyalty.

Legitimate: Legitimate power is rooted in titles and is employed when couples use their labels as husband, wife, boyfriend, or girl-friend to define relationship boundaries and rules. Legitimate power is most commonly used in monogamous relationships to safeguard against infidelity and within marriages to ensure equal access to children and financial assets. A major benefit that comes with legitimate power is the exclusivity of having a monogamous sexual partner. A closed, monogamous relationship is when sexual intimacy is only given and received between two exclusive inti-mate partners. Legitimate power makes the management of sex a mutual responsibility for both intimate partners. Therapy helps couples identify procedures they can implement in order to work through feelings that block the use of their legitimate power.

Why Therapy Helps

When couples develop distorted views of their relationship roles and responsibilities, they lose meaning for their legitimate power, which originates from the titles they define during different stages of the relationship. Therapy assists couples by helping them define their ideal functions as each other's intimate partner, so their legitimate power is clarified.

During the initial meeting with one couple, I asked them how they defined their titles in the relationship, and they both responded with gestures of uncertainty. I then asked them if they have agreed to be each other's exclusive sources for physical and sexual intimacy. The female responded yes, and the male partner responded no. We then proceeded to define how their relationship evolved and located the point in time where they became unclear of their relationship status. The male partner stated that they decided to take a break from the relationship and assumed that meant he was free to pursue other sexual partners. The female partner viewed the break as a brief period of not spending as much time together, but never internalized it as an open invitation to sleep with other people. She then began to clarify that during their break period she was still continuing to have sex exclusively with her boyfriend, because they were still intimate partners.

Therapy provides couples with the clarity they need so they can effectively use verbal communication to determine if their legitimate power is still enforceable. In the example above, the couple suffered from improper communication, which led to the female partner deploying legitimate power she no longer had.

Therapy assists couples by providing them with a variety of processes including effective communication, relationship mapping, and role clarification which are used to restore legitimate power.

The Four Tools Needed for Intimate Partners to Make Joint Decision

1. *Needs:* A necessary requirement for the sustainability of health, safety, or fulfillment within the confines of the intimate relationship.
2. *Wants*: A desired object or experience that will provide one or both partners with gratification but is not necessary to maintain relationship satisfaction.
3. *Purpose*: The motivation for why one or both partners desires a specific need or want.
4. *Process:* The course of action that intimate partners use to determine if a need or want will be met.

Arguments and Fights

Each intimate partner's unique worldview is shaped by their past and current life experiences. In an attempt to convince their significant other to see the world through their own lens, couples will engage in arguments. Arguments are healthy exchanges of thoughts and ideas that are driven by each partner's level of passion for the topic being debated. When both partners take turns speaking and listening, arguments can be healthy, persuasive conversations that couples use to settle disputes, make joint decisions, and express their points of view. Arguments become problematic when partners aren't able to hear each other properly. When this happens, couples transition from arguing to fighting. A fight is intended to produce a loser and a winner.

The main goal of an argument is to identify a mutual inter-section for both partners' thoughts, feelings, and ideas. Once each partner has respectfully expressed themselves, the couple can move forward with creating one harmonious perspective. When partners approach a disagreement with the intention of winning or beating each other, then they are engaging in a fight. The main factor to be aware of that causes couples to stop hearing each other during arguments is tone. Every part of the argument or persuasive conversation is important, but how it starts holds the most value, because it sets the tone for how the discussion will play out. Tone is impacted by the attitude each partner brings into the conversation and influences the volume used to transmit verbal messages. Healthy arguments start when partners communicate in a tone that displays a desire to engage. Partners who are calm and use respectful tones make it easier to start the argument in a noncombative fashion. The opposite would be true for partners who have an aggressive and demanding approach, which can cause defensiveness at the outset of the argument. Good tone also has to be coupled with good timing, waiting for an appropriate time to engage in arguments that have the ability to conclude with each partner feeling heard. Finding the right time to engage in an argument is important because partners may need to prepare themselves to listen, or might not be in the right mind-set for a constructive argument.

Why Therapy Helps

Couples will seek therapy because they do not know how to argue without transitioning the dialogue into a fight. Fights are more likely to develop when the couple loses sight of purpose or forgets why they began the argument to start with. At this point, they are driven by heightened emotions and start to hurt each other. These exchanges quickly develop when either partner feels attacked during the conversation.

When partners feel attacked, they will automatically start to defend themselves. Defensiveness takes the form of shooting back insults, placing blame, or shutting down and refusing to engage. These behavior responses are taught through observations and past experiences. In therapy, couples are shown how to process their style of fighting and are introduced to steps they can apply in order to rewire any of their faulty training. Oftentimes, intimate partners are taught at an early age that if someone hits them, they should hit them back. The problem with this methodology is that when we form intimate relationships, this eye-for-an-eye approach produces two people who can no longer see. Couples become blinded by anger, pain, and rage. These negative emotions drive couples to hurt each other, which goes against the premise of establishing a healthy intimate relationship. A therapist can help couples identify when they start to feel attacked during an argument and how to express their feelings. This is done through a variety of techniques that allow couples to revisit their arrangements in the controlled setting of the therapy room. This approach is similar to how an athlete watches game footage to see what mistakes they made so they can correct the actions during the next game. Therapy helps partners with processing their arguments, so they can practice having persuasive conversations that sustain respect and conclude with resolutions. Partners have to learn each other's triggers and make a choice to not purposefully hurt each other when they argue their thoughts, feelings, or emotions.

The Four T's of Arguments Between Intimate Partners

1. ***Timing:*** The moment when partners become triggered by an activating event, thought, or emotion that leads to the start of an argument despite the setting or environment.

2. ***Tone:*** The attitudes and communication styles projected and received by partners who engage in planned and unplanned arguments, emotionally charged dialogues, or conversations.

3. ***Topic:*** The subject, event, need, want, or thing that provoked some emotion, thought, or belief within one or both partners which acted as the catalyst for the argument.

4. ***Triumph:*** The conclusion of the argument which can be a solution, resolution, compromise, or a result that leads both partners toward adopting a joint perspective on how they will move forward together in the relationship.

Intimate Disconnections

Intimate relationships are established when partners choose to build an alliance that stems from a mutual attraction for each other. The fondness that keeps couples together is called intimacy. Intimacy is the heartbeat that supports the life of the relationship and grows the connection between partners. Any act, event, or moment that facilitates connection can been defined as "intimacy." It is common for couples to interchangeably refer to intimacy as sex, but sex is only one act that yields closeness between partners. The act of sexual intercourse is a type of physical intimacy, but couples more frequently engage in emotional, intellectual, and recreational exchanges that produce connection. Couples can develop problems with intimacy when they experience less time together or when they lack the intentionality required to create moments that generate closeness. This is why couples who have recently become new parents or encounter life transitions that reduce their time together oftentimes report feeling less intimate. Couples have to spend time together sharing physical, emotional, intellectual, and recreational exchanges if they want to sustain high levels of intimacy.

The Four Types of Intimate Exchanges that Grow Connection

Physical intimacy consists of all forms of bodily contact shared between partners, including touching, kissing, cuddling, and sexual intercourse. Issues associated with physical intimacy can occur when partners do not feel safe, heard, understood or cared for. However, in this section, I am going to focus on couples that lack physical intimacy because they do not feel heard by each other. Partners who do not know how to effectively communicate how they feel and what they need have the most difficulty sustaining physical intimacy. The need for physical intimacy originates from our childhood family experience and past experiences that pro-duce either negative or positive stimuli associated with physical touch. Partners who grew up encountering limited or no physical affection may not place a high value on touch. However, the opposite can also be true—partners who come from families that did not embrace a lot of physical affection may desire it more because they felt deprived as a child. It is important during the courtship phase to assess your partner's degree of physical intimacy needs, which include the types of contact and the frequency in which they are desired. The quality and frequency of physical intimacy is a common concern couples seek to treat in therapy. These issues can be present from the inception of the relationship or can transpire later. They are made worse when couples do not effectively talk about what they need, and are unable to devise a plan to ensure both partners' needs for physical intimacy are satisfied.

Why Therapy Helps

During the initial phase of therapy, counselors are constantly probing to identify the origins of the problems brought in by the couple. A good way to find out more about this is to inquire about the couple's most recent sexual experience. This question is critical, because sex is an important identifier in determining degrees of physical closeness between intimate partners. Some of the most common reasons couples stop engaging in sex include health and human growth issues and attachment wounds. Attachment wounds are injuries to the relationship that develop from events in which one partner experienced emotional hurt caused by the other. Couples can inflict attachment injuries on each other and be unaware of the damage produced. This happens when couples choose to ignore changes in the relationship by avoiding the hard conversations that give room for each partner to express how they feel.

Therapy supports couples to have these challenging conversations that are required in order to initiate the healing process. The only way couples can mend their attachment injuries is by expressing how they feel so their partner can gain a better understanding for their hurt. Once the therapist has successfully facilitated the reconciliation process, the couple is then ready to move toward learning how to be physically intimate again. Certain types of physical intimacy, such as engaging in sexual intercourse, are challenging for couples to reengage in after long hiatuses. Couples will experience mild anxiety created by the flashbacks of rejection they encountered during the time their relationship was in a bad place. Therapy helps couples move past their hurt and reestablish physical intimacy. The therapist guides this process by teaching partners how to communicate their feelings, embrace forgiveness, and rehabilitate the relationship so it can once again support all forms of physically intimate expressions.

Emotional intimacy is experienced when partners feel accepted, secure, cared for, understood, and completely free to be them-selves. This occurs when couples engage in the exchange of words and actions that support these feelings. Emotional intimacy varies in degrees but is the most common form of intimate expression, because there are so many ways in which it can happen. Anything from telling your partner you were thinking about them to some-thing as great to asking for their hand in marriage can account for an expression of emotional intimacy. Couples develop problems with emotional intimacy when they begin to lose interest in each other. Staying interested in your partner is work that can only be sustained by constantly inquiring about how they feel, what they need, and what they want. Feelings, needs, and wants are always changing and will remain the moving target that drives connection between intimate partners.

Some partners may need an increase in verbal affirmation during periods of stress or personal doubt to feel emotionally connected. Other partners may need doses of emotional expressions multiple times a day to feel secure in the intimate relationship. Similar to physical intimacy, emotional intimacy needs differ from partner to partner, which makes it an important topic to assess when developing a relationship. If one or both partners do not first feel secure in themselves, they will never be able to truly fulfill each other's emotional intimacy needs. This is because emotional intimacy stems from feelings of acceptance and recognition. It is essential for intimate partners to supplement each other's need for approval, but they should not exclusively bear the weight of being each other's sole source of validation. Healthy emotionally intimate relationships are founded by two emotionally stable partners who come together to form a mutually expressive union. This requires the presence of emotional equality, which is developed independently of the relationship. If it is known that one or both partners has low self-esteem, feels lesser in value, or sees their worth as minimal, then individual therapy would be recommended first or in conjunction to couples counseling to treat emotional intimacy needs.

Why Therapy Helps

Therapy helps couples by helping them identify individual emotional needs and expectations. Couples will enter therapy expecting their partner to know what they want, and can experience an emotional letdown in the event that they don't receive what they expected. Some partners may desire more attention on special occasions such as anniversaries, birthdays, and holidays, in order to feel more emotionally connected. In therapy, the couple is able to share how they felt when one partner either forgot about a special occasion or failed to meet their partner's expectations. The therapist validates the hurt partner's feelings and helps the under-performer by assisting them in devising strategies to ensure they can meet expectations the next time. Some partners want more energy to be placed in daily interactions that can communicate emotional expressions. A therapist can assist with this by helping partners learn how to engage in deeper conversations, facilitate opportunities for emotional check-ins, or demonstrate small acts that express care. Therapy can get couples back on track to feeling emotionally connected through the use of a variety of interventions. Therapy works at getting couples emotionally balanced when both partners come in with a mutual desire to demonstrate their love for each other.

Intellectual intimacy grows the more couples learn about each other. This form of intimacy is associated with the knowledge each partner gains about the other's hobbies, likes, dislikes, goals, and life dreams.

Couples develop issues with intellectual intimacy when they stop learning about each other. Couples will constantly change during the course of the intimate relationship, and keeping up with your partner's ever changing interests takes work but can be exciting. Change supports monogamy by keeping the relationship with one person fresh. Every time our partner goes through a new phase in life and takes us along for the ride with them, a deeper level of intellectual intimacy is achieved. After my wife and I had our first child, she decided to adopt healthier eating and living habits. I was a fellow passenger alongside her in this excursion through the jungle of natural healthcare practices. We read books about juicing, raw food diets, and the benefits of natural hygienic products. I accompanied her on trips to the gym and countless rides to the farmers' market. I was even brave enough to watch as she went through with her "big chop"—when she cut off much of her hair after she decided to go with a natural style that excluded harsh chemicals designed to straighten curls. Our intellectual connection grew through the process of becoming healthier together. We learned more about each other's likes and dislikes pertaining to food, fitness, and healthcare practices. When couples decide to journey through different phases of life together, learning about new things and each other in the process, their intellectual intimacy deepens. Intellectual intimacy requires couples to consistently work to hear each other as they learn about their partner's ever-changing personality, expectations, needs, and wants.

Why Therapy Helps

During the initial phase of therapy, couples may reveal that they are starting to feel distant from each other. After exploring areas around sex and emotional connection, the therapist will ask questions about the couple's ability to connect intellectually. Couples easily forget that in order to stay intellectually connected, they have to work toward sustaining the same intensity they had at the beginning of the relationship. Naturally, when couples start dating, their curiosity for each other is heightened and, over time, the elasticity of knowledge partners have for each other is worn down.

Therapists help couples reestablish intellectual intimacy with the application of interventions such as Love Maps. Renowned author, researcher, and therapist John Gottman wrote about the power of Love Maps in his book *The Seven Principles of Making Marriage Work*. Gottman and his team developed Love Maps after conducting over thirty years of research with couples to identify questions, activities, and games that assist intimate partners with securing their intellectual connection. Couples turn to therapy to process the thoughts, emotions, and feelings that develop while constructing their Love Maps together. Therapy operates as a laboratory for the experiment of reconnection to be proven and tested. The hypothesis is that both partners desire to restore their connectivity, but sometimes partners learn that their connection has a short circuit. A short circuit is a lower resistant connection between two partners, or a loss of energy. As a result, one partner may be applying more energy to connect, and the other partner chooses not to engage. Over time, the desperate efforts from the one partner trying to connect will end up destroying the relationship, because they will feel rejected and unwanted. This adverse result can happen because couples have learned that their relationship has run its course. When one or both partners no longer desire to make the effort of continuing to bond, their intellectual intimacy can die.

Therapy helps unveil each partner's desire to connect or disconnect from the relationship. Couples who embrace the interventions and enjoy creating their Love Maps are able to grow. Partners who no longer desire to remain in the relationship will no longer make an effort to learn new things about their significant other. Intellectual intimacy is one of the major sources of nutrients that relationships depend on to sustain themselves and function properly. Therapy gives couples the needed supplements to boost intellectual intimacy so their relationship can thrive. In some cases, one or both partners craving more intellectual intimacy may be blocked by past hurt or attachment wounds. In therapy, if these couples choose to do the work, they can learn to forgive each other and securely move back into a space that supports the growth of intellectual intimacy. Therapy helps couples that need to heal before they can regain connection and couples that have forgotten how to connect.

Recreational intimacy is created when couples engage in shared activities that produce mutual feelings of euphoria. The premise is that by spending time creating fun-filled memories, couples become closer. Intimate partners develop issues around recreational intimacy when they do not intentionally plan time to participate in leisure experiences that both partners enjoy. These problems are exacerbated when one partner plans a date that only includes things they like. When a partner fails to consider the other's interests, it demonstrates neutrality instead of equality. Recreational intimacy is ignited by the mutual feelings of gratification both partners experience while indulging in a shared event. If an activity or outing does not suit both partners, then the event will create disconnection because one partner will not feel like their needs and wants were met.

Partners who want to create recreational intimacy have to both be involved in the planning process. This can be achieved with each partner providing their consent on all the itinerary items prior to approval. Couples will commonly make the mistake of letting one partner solely plan the event. This stifles the couple's ability to maximize their connection, because the planning process is the first phase of recreational intimacy. While couples are planning, they are able to visualize the future experience, and that activates feelings of euphoria prior to engaging in the moment. By planning the trip or activity together the couple can also rest assured that each partner gets what they want and limits the risk of displeasure. Recreational intimacy is activated when couples spend time engaging in activities, events, and outings that generate feelings of euphoria in both partners.

Why Therapy Helps

Couples do not have to like the same things in order to sustain a healthy intimate relationship. One partner may find peace on a hike in the woods, while the other might find relaxation from watching a movie on the couch. Some couples both enjoy out-door activities and the sedentary moments of watching television but have a hard time deciding when to engage in the experiences together. Couples use therapy to get on the same page so they can effectively plan moments that foster recreational intimacy. One partner may prefer not to engage with the other during a certain activity, and this can create problems if their partner wants to share that moment with them.

I recall hearing a female partner during therapy express how she loved going to the gym but felt like the experience was tainted when her boyfriend accompanied her. She elaborated by articulating how he always felt the need to critique her form, and that made her feel belittled. Even though her boyfriend's intention was to be helpful, it was not received that way by the female partner. I asked the female partner about other times she felt like this and she stated those feelings existed any time he tried to offer his suggestions. The dialogue began to open up into other areas of the couple's relationship. The boyfriend learned that, because his partner grew up with critical parents, she learned to internalize all suggestions as criticism. Slowly and over time, the couple had stopped engaging in recreational activities like bowling, miniature golf, and roller-skating because the female partner no longer desired to hear her boyfriend's suggestions on how to improve her form. Therapy provided a safe place for her to share these feelings for the first time. Her boyfriend was empathetic after listening to his girlfriend's feelings and he identified that his behavior mimicked his father's. He shared how, whenever he and his dad participated in activities together, the fun was sucked out of it because the moment quickly turned into a training session. Therapy assisted him with gaining a new perspective to approaching recreational activities with his girlfriend. Moreover, he developed a heightened awareness for all his suggestions. He learned to ask for his girlfriend's permission prior to providing comments that could be taken as unsolicited criticisms. Over time, the couple was able to reengage in more recreational activities together because both partners felt mutual levels of satisfaction. Therapy helps couples flush out emotional clogs that block recreational intimacy from flowing. The therapist navigates through tough conversations with the couple while exposing emotions that derive from their past history and prior experiences. Intimate partners are able to find the key feelings that unlock doors and reopen recreational intimacy.

The Four Tools Used to Build Intimacy

1. ***Connection:*** The process of attaching to your partner by intentionally performing actions that satisfy their need to feel accepted, desired, and valued.

2. **Deed:** An action that fulfills a desire and creates a stronger relationship connection.

3. **Desire:** The willingness to fulfill your intimate partner's needs and wants in exchange for the satisfaction of knowing you made them happy.

4. **Vulnerability:** Making the choice to willingly share your feelings with your intimate partner despite the risk that they could reject you or not approve of how you feel.

Barriers That Block Intimate Partners from Feeling Heard

In order for couples to properly send and receive messages, intimate partners have to first make sure their lines of communication are free and clear. Communication pathways used to transport messages do not work properly when intimate partners display signs of defensiveness, become distracted, make assumptions, or pass judgments on each other. The following four barriers have to be identified and treated before intimate partners can feel heard by each other:

- Defensiveness
- Distractions
- Assumptions
- Judgments

Defensiveness

When couples feel they are under attack from their partner they become defensive. Intimate partners naturally engage in defensive behaviors the same way our bodies organically respond to infections. We are equipped with emotional defense systems that are activated when we start to feel under siege by any perceived threat, including those that come from our intimate partner. When our partner surrounds us with questions or comments that assault our character, beliefs, and viewpoints, we fire back. We use an artillery of reflective comments, explanations, and justifications to ward off our partner's attacks. After the dust has settled, both partners leave the engagement feeling wounded and unheard. These engagements continue to come about whenever either partner attempts to transmit a message designed to share how they feel or what they need for the relationship to improve. Defensive behaviors that commonly block partners from hearing each other are deflecting, explaining, safeguarding, and justifying. All of these behavior responses prevent partners from properly transmitting messages and have the potential to activate fights.

Why Therapy Helps

Intimate partners feel threatened by unique triggers that induce defensive behaviors. Therapists help couples by identifying the underlining emotions that make partners feel unsafe. Once a partner feels threatened, they stop listening and seek to only protect and defend themselves. The threats experienced by partners are often connected to family history and past traumas. A husband who becomes triggered when his wife expresses disappointment in him flashes back to the person he was in adolescence who always got into trouble. He starts to tell his side of the story, but that only provokes his wife to feel more unheard. Once he acknowledges she is not listening, he then begins to blame her for being a perfectionist who sweats the small stuff, similar to his parents. She is disgusted by his remarks and shuts down. Both partners exit the exchange feeling hurt and the issue goes unresolved.

Therapy helps couples find the triggering emotions so partners can rewrite their rules of engagement. In therapy, the couple from my example identified the origins for their defensive behaviors so they could send fewer triggering messages that had a better chance of being received during moments of conflict. When their next argument occurred, the female partner started the dialogue with a validation that proved to her husband she was mindful he does do things that please her. She said, "Last night you cooked an amazing dinner but this morning when I woke up your under-wear was sitting on the floor beside the clothes hamper." Instead of instantly feeling like he can do no good, the husband is able to better digest his wife's complaint because it followed a validation of an action she appreciated. Therapists help couples better send messages so they can avoid triggering emotional landmines that produce feelings of defensiveness inside their partner.

The Four Common Types of Defensiveness

Deflecting: The process of redirecting fault, blame, or responsibility back onto your intimate partner while they are attempting to communicate an issue, complaint, or need that has gone unmet. Example:

> *"You are not perfect either. If I recall, you were late picking the kids up from school last week too."*

Explaining: Quickly providing your intimate partner with a reason for why you failed to meet their expectation prior to hearing their thoughts, feelings, and emotions pertaining to the situation. Example:

> *"Before you finish talking, let me explain. I was late because my boss called me into his office to discuss a promotion."*

Safeguarding: Providing your partner with facts or evidence for why your action was not that bad, instead of taking responsibility for what you did. Example:

> *"I have been on time all this week and last week. This was the first time I was late this month—give me a break!"*

Justifying: Providing your intimate partner with an excuse or reason to why you did or didn't do something instead of seeking ways to reconcile the situation by listening to how they feel. Example:

"So which one was more important: me being on time or learning about an opportunity to make more money?"

Distractions

Couples have to learn how to reduce and eliminate all distractions in order to successfully hear each other. Internal and external distractions block couples from transmitting signals back and forth.

Internal distractions are the feelings and emotions that give way to our thoughts. Thoughts that are not controlled can interfere with the transmission of messages, similar to how weeds take over a lawn that is not treated to prevent them. When we listen to our intimate partner, we have to silence our minds and control our thoughts from running rampant. Couples often argue because one of them became distracted during the conversation. The receiver may have been so immersed in their own thoughts that they failed to hear the message. The sender might have thought what to say but was so distracted by the running list in their head, they forgot to actually speak the words they intended to. In these instances, it is important to be patient with our intimate partner and simply ask them to repeat what was said. If this practice becomes a habit, then it is apparent one or both partners are not intently listening and could be suffering from internal distractions.

External distractions are any physical thing that prevents the transmission, receipt, or transcription of messages sent between intimate partners. These days, the use of technology is the most common form of external distraction mentioned by couples I treat in therapy. Partners regularly describe how their significant other does not hear them because they are distracted by a cell phone, gaming system, television, or computer. If your partner feels like they are competing against your media devices for your attention, then external distractions are creating communication problems in your relationship. When using technology to communicate, messages have a way of not always being sent. Depending on the strength of the cellular signal, phone calls can be dropped and text messages can go unreceived. Text messages and emails add an additional obstacle because they lack tone and are subject to interpretation by the reader. For this reason, couples should refrain from texting or emailing about emotionally charged content. Internal and external distractions are inevitable, but couples can learn how to manage interruptions so both partners feel heard.

Why Therapy Helps

All intimate relationships are tested by distractions and it is unrealistic to expect your partner to give you their undivided attention one hundred percent of the time. Therapy helps couples to identify and reduce distractions that get in the way of partners feeling heard by each other. Therapists will first assess the couple's interactions by asking questions pertaining to their environment, routines, and habits in order to track communication sequences. This is happening in real time as well, and the best data is collected while the couples are speaking aloud to one another. Therapists operate like a symphony conductor, pointing out each partner's communication mishap with a quest for meaning. When one partner abruptly interrupts the other in midsentence, the therapist pauses the dialogue to shed light on the distracting behavior. As couples continue the progress, the therapist probes deeper to learn about other times one or both partners did not feel heard due to distractions. Couples use the safe space in therapy to share how they felt unheard or that they were playing second fiddle to their partner's cell phone, gaming sys-tem, work, or even their children. Once the awareness of these dis-tractions occurs, the therapist steps in to assist with heightening the feelings of contentment so they can be absorbed by the receiving partner. Therapists operate as conductors of emotions—both good and bad—because partners who really care for one another will use opportunities in therapy to apologize, forgive, and save each other once they realize the origins of the issues they are having.

The Four Types of Communication Distractions

Internal: Thoughts, feelings, and emotions that consume the listener and disrupt them from properly receiving the messages that are sent by the intimate partner.

External: People, places, and things that prevent couples from instant or scheduled engagement in verbal or nonverbal communication pertaining to how they feel about a topic or subject of importance.

Interruption: Cognitive and external distractions that abruptly appear and lead to the premature ending or delayed continuation of a conversation and expression of emotions, thoughts, or ideas.

Triggers: Flashbacks, accusations, thoughts, or feelings that arise in the middle of a conversation with your intimate partner that prevent or disrupt continued listening and processing.

Assumptions

I often witness intimate partners bringing assumptions into therapy. Assumptions create huge barriers that prevent partners from being heard. Due to the fact that assumptions are often wrong, they have the ability to inaccurately depict how an event will turn out and can falsify what our intimate partner is thinking and feeling.

Assumptions tend to be incorrect because they are created from our negative thoughts or worst-case scenarios constructed from external influences. We hear news about something bad happening and then apply the potential of the same event occurring in our life, which is how assumptions are birthed. For example, you learn that your friend found their partner cheating on social media, and this news prompts you to monitor your partner's social media activity. You begin to question every picture "like," tweet, or person they decide to follow. The first time your partner comes home late or they take their phone with them into the bathroom, you assume they are now cheating on you. This assumption continues to be fueled daily each time you talk with your friend, who constantly shares details about how they were deceived. I person-ally recall a period when my wife was fixated on watching reality television and developed assumptions that stemmed from the characters on the shows. One example that we joke about to this day was when she came home one morning after working third shift and found the pillow covers on the couch removed. The night prior, our son became sick and vomited all over the couch. I removed the pillow covers and placed them in the washing machine, but did not replace them before my wife got home. When she entered the house, she immediately assumed I was cleaning the pillows to coverup a trace of another woman who was there while she was at work. Her assumption that I was cheating stemmed from a story line she watched on one of the reality shows. One of the characters was notorious for cheating on his spouse while his wife was out of town. My wife allowed the television show to fuel a false assumption which in turn impaired her judgment of my character. Her assumption, which was the worst-case scenario for why the pillow covers were removed, also blocked her ability to hear the true reason. We were able to quickly identify the origin of my wife's false assumption and moved on from this event. Some couples are not as fortunate and need help identifying and dissolving the sources of their false assumptions. Assumptions for many couples are a major source of relationship conflict because they prevent partners from hearing each other.

Why Therapy Helps

Our perceptions can become our realities over time if we are not exposed to different influential factors designed to reconfigure insight and awareness. The same way our bodies become what we put into them, our minds create the pictures from the information we expose them to. Couples therapy helps by exposing each partner to different ways of thinking so they can produce a clearer picture for how they fit into each other's lives together. Assumptions are treated at their origins, which define the way each partner chooses to process or think about themselves, each other, and the intimate relationship as a whole. Therapists explore each partner's family of origin and other factors that generate the production of their assumptions. This process is designed to better help couples expose their blind spots or faulty thinking, which have the potential to create distorted assumptions.

Distorted assumptions are the runaway thoughts that drive the worst-case scenarios in our heads. Couples then project these negative pictures onto either themselves, their partner, or the relationship. Therapists lead couples towards healing by asking questions and applying interventions that assist with calibrating how couples absorb and process information. The therapist does not produce change by solving a specific issue or processing a set of facts. Instead, therapists operate by helping partners alter the rules of engagement for themselves and the relationship. Changing the rules individually can manifest as one partner suggesting that the other reduces their exposure to sources that have been linked to manufacturing distorted assumptions. As a couple, it can also help for both partners to write down their assumptions prior to speaking or acting on them. By writing the assumptions out, each partner is given the time to slow down and process the information in their heads before speaking them aloud or making a decision. This intervention works to rewrite the rules of engagement and is designed to create systematic changes. Therapy helps couples man-age assumptions by teaching each partner how to slow down and put their thoughts in a holding space before handing them over. The additional time for processing reduces irrationality, defensiveness, and negative outbursts. From attending therapy, couples are able to stop their assumptions from becoming dams that block the flow of communication. When couples allow assumptions to snowball into truths, neither partner will feel heard.

The Four Misrepresentations That Fuel Assumptions

Information: Incorrect news that is based on worst-case scenarios and derives from sources such as family, friends, or selected media outlets.

History: Past experiences, events, or information that reinforce negative thoughts and beliefs regarding an occurrence or situation involving your intimate partner.

Interpretations: Translations of events, scenarios, or actions pertaining to your intimate partner based on bits and pieces of information that are used to support negative thoughts and beliefs.

Mind Reading: Operating under the belief that you can accurately identify what your intimate partner is thinking and feeling without them telling you.

Judgments

Morality is taught during the earliest stages of human growth and development. Both our caretakers and our life experiences teach us lessons that we use to establish a personal rating system for what we perceive to be right and wrong. From these teachable moments, we develop personal values, beliefs, and an ethical code. We then use our ethical code as a measuring tool throughout our life to help judge people, decisions, and outcomes. It is common for couples to stop listening to each other when they feel their partner's words challenge their personal beliefs. Displaying this form of judgment during verbal dialogues blocks your partner from feeling heard. Our "judgment"— or what we define as right or wrong—does not change when we choose to listen to our partner speak. Listening to our partner does not condone their words and does not mean we are agreeing with them or what they think. Instead, empathetically listening to our partner builds trust and enables them to be more receptive to hearing our responses. The act of judging our partner while they are attempting to transmit verbal messages can easily cause them to shut down. When our significant other no longer feels safe to share, or believes their words are not getting through, verbal communication ceases.

Why Therapy Helps

A common communication barrier that blocks intimate partners from feeling heard are judgments made during conversations involving major decisions. Choices that have a mutual impact on the couple or the relationship create a scenario where partners may more readily inflict judgements. In therapy, couples are provided with tools they can use to share their thoughts, concerns, and opinions when discussing topics that challenge each partner's belief systems. The therapist teaches the couple how to use active listening, emotional identification, and techniques to help them see their partner's perspective, so they can transmit their feelings with-out sounding judgmental. Couples get the opportunity to practice these skills under the guidance of a trained communication specialist and then are assigned tasks between sessions that assist them with integrating the techniques into their natural dialogues. Over the course of attending therapy, both partners will become efficient at listening and speaking without judgment.

The Four Skills Couples Learn from Therapy to Reduce Judgments

1. *Active Listening:* The process of asking your intimate partner open-ended questions in order to affirm, reflect, and summarize what they are saying and feeling.
2. *Emotional Identification:* Allowing your intimate partner to share their unique perspective as their truth, while seeking to find the emotions they are attempting to communicate.
3. *Perspective Taking:* Choosing to step outside of your own thoughts, beliefs, and viewpoints in order to experience how your intimate partner sees the world.
4. *Responsiveness:* Acknowledging that you heard what your partner said by responding with verbal and nonverbal communication cues designed to confirm you are listening.

Chapter 3

REASON THREE:
TO FEEL UNDERSTOOD

Feeling understood by your intimate partner creates security, because. When your intimate partner understands you, it is easier for you both to develop mutual interest and concerns, because your words, thoughts, and feelings are in alignment. Couples with a greater understanding for one another take on shared responsibilities that are assigned based on the acknowledgment of each partner's unique skills and talents. When understanding is present between intimate partners, they can lean on each other with a sense of dependability and trust. Robert Weiss's Theory of Social Provisions outlines six interpersonal needs, and claims that people meet these needs through the attainment of multiple types of relationships or from one primary relationship. These six interpersonal needs can be met within intimate relationships when partners take the time to understand each other's needs and wants.

Meeting Interpersonal Needs By Way of Feeling Understood
(Weiss's Social Provisions)

Provision 1: Senses of Safety and Security When partners form an intimate relationship, they adopt behaviors, roles, and commitments in order to coexist as a unit. Taking the time to learn what your partner requires based on past hurts or present needs produces a sense of safety and security. When a new boyfriend takes the time to understand that his girlfriend was cheated on in the past by a man who worked late hours, he will be more likely to meet her request of making check-in calls on the nights he has to work over-time, so she can feel secure. This same girlfriend takes the time to understand that in her boyfriend's past relationship, he didn't feel appreciated, so she constantly validates him for the check-in calls and tells him how safe he makes her feel in the relationship.

Provision 2: Mutual Interest and Concerns Intimate partners will experience an increase in mutual interest and concerns as they work to fit into each other's lives. These interests and concerns are both retroactive and current, based on the course of each partner's life up until the point the intimate relationship was established. For example, if your partner has a preexisting medical condition that has concerned them their entire life, it will become a mutual concern of yours too as the relationship builds. Partners who understand each other inherit mutual interest and concerns because they learn to see equal value in meeting their partner's needs and wants.

Provision 3: Acknowledgment of Skills and Abilities Couples who seek to gain the most out of their relationship understand the value of working smarter and not harder. They acknowledge each other's unique individual skill sets and then divvy up relationship responsibilities based on who is good at what. Each partner should desire to bring a specific skill set or ability into the relationship. Think about it like preparing your best dish for the church or office potluck lunch. For these couples to acknowledge their individual skills and abilities, they have to gain a strong understanding for each other, which comes from spending time together and creating shared experiences.

Provision 4: Sharing Responsibility for Each Other's Well-Being
The ability to care for your intimate partner's health, happiness, goal attainment, and overall well-being is present in relationships that stem from understanding. These couples understand that there is value in covering each other's blind spots. In intimate relationships, this may look like the partner who is more organized choosing to take on the responsibility of managing medication regimens, meal planning, and scheduling doctor's appointments for themselves and their intimate partner.

Provision 5: Receive Advice and Assistance A couple who understands that their intimate partner has their best interests in mind will be more receptive to embracing advice and assistance. Understanding breeds trust, because it requires that couples take the time to learn their partner's good and bad behaviors based on personal experiences. This is evident when a wife tells her husband of several years he may want to pause and wait a day before he sends an email to his boss because she knows he does not always use the best words when he is angry. She does not tell her husband what to do because he doesn't like orders but, instead, she simply advises him on a method that can produce the desired outcome he wants. He knows his wife understands him because of countless arguments they experienced when he projected hurtful words toward her because he was angry in the moment, so he trusts her advice to wait a day before sharing his feelings with his boss.

Provision 6: Reliability Despite Circumstances When couples understand their partner's needs, they will find a way to be available despite the circumstance. These partners make sure they show up every time because they understand the value of their word and the commitment they provide to their partner. When committed couples have an understanding of what their partner needs, they no long try to meet each other's expectations, but instead they make sure they strive to exceed them.

The Four C's of Understanding Within Intimate Relationships

1. **Context**: The assessment of a situation or action based on the unique perspective of your intimate partner (i.e., seeing it the way they see it).
2. **Consideration**: Comparing context and intended out-comes in order to gain a better understanding of why your intimate partner thinks, feels, or acts in a particular way.
3. **Comprehension**: Examining past outcomes and experiences to gain a complete understanding regarding why your intimate partner thinks, feels, and acts the way they do.
4. **Confirmation**: Obtaining validation from your intimate partner that you understand them based on your ability to accurately decode their words, actions, and feelings.

Problems that Develop When Intimate Partners Do Not Feel Understood

When intimate partners are unable to comprehend each other's words, actions, and feelings, major core relationship problems can form. The four major relationship problems that develop when misunderstandings linger are feelings of loneliness, a lack of commitment, a reduction in relationship satisfaction, and difficulties parenting.

- Loneliness
- Lack of Commitment
- Reduction in Relationship Satisfaction
- Parenting Issues

Loneliness

I hear clients express feelings of loneliness in their relationship when their intimate partner becomes physically, emotionally, spiritually, intellectually, or socially unavailable. These types of breeches in connection suddenly develop and become reinforced as partners learn how to satisfy their connectional needs independently of the relationship. Loneliness spreads like a form of cancer that mutates healthy relationship cells and causes an increase in negative feelings and perceptions, an inability to properly cope with emotions, and opens the floodgates for risky behaviors. These responses by partners who feel lonely within their intimate relationship are based on a paper written by Deniz Cosan titled "An Evolution of Loneliness" which was published by the *European Proceedings of Social and Behavioral Sciences.*

Negative Feelings Partners who feel lonely within their intimate relationship will also inherit accompanied feelings of rejection, boredom, unhappiness, and anger. These negative feelings are a byproduct of physical and emotional needs of intimacy and connection not being met. Feelings of loneliness tend to stem from rejection because something is preventing or "rejecting" connection from happening between intimate partners. Physical rejections occur when partners are unable to see each other or spend time together. Physical barriers are the most common forms of rejection, but not all rejections are based on the inability to physically connect. Partners who are in the military, travel often, or who work in isolated environments are more susceptible to experiencing intensifying feelings of loneliness. The negative feelings that stem from loneliness will continue to intensify over time if partners do not alter their relationship to accommodate each other's intimate needs. If action is not taken, then partners will begin to develop negative perceptions.

Negative Perceptions Lonely people are reported to be more negative because they are hurting from feeling rejected, abandoned, or unwanted. The saying "hurt people hurt other people" sums up that individuals tend to project their negative feelings onto their loved ones. Partners who are hurt due to feeling lonely will start to see life through a lens that is tainted by skepticism, uncertainty, and disapproval of their intimate partner. Being the mate of some-one who feels lonely in the relationship, one might experience their partner slipping into reclusive behaviors, being less affectionate, going through mood swings, or might even be on the receiving end of false accusations of infidelity. In a relationship involving a lonely partner, one might also feel like it is impossible to please their partner, even when they are together. These negative perceptions put a strain on the intimate relationship, making it hard for the couple to properly cope with problems.

Inability to Cope with Problems All couples experience problems or conflict, but in healthy relationships there is a strong immune system that comes from both partners feeling like their needs are being met. This immune system of care that is used to ward off negative feelings in the midst of moments of conflict is disabled in relationships where partners feel lonely. The inability to cope with problems is more prevalent in relationships with lonely-feeling partners, because the couples start to lose hope and the value of the relationship is lessened. When relationship value starts to plummet, couples experience a depletion in the desire to communicate, spend time together, and demonstrate empathy. It is inevitable that, over time, the buildup of negative feelings and perspectives and the inability to cope with problems will produce risky behaviors that can deplete the relationship.

Risky Behaviors Unreconcilable actions, such as physical abuse and infidelity, are two risky behaviors that are prevalent in relationships with intimate partners who feel lonely. Intimate partners who have a history of displaying violent behaviors will commonly respond with aggression when their feelings of loneliness reach a boiling point. Partners who are less confrontational will take a more passive approach at attempting to get their need for connection met. The lonely-feeling partner may choose to establish complementary relationships with other people who are not their intimate partner. These complementary relationships become risky when they press against the boundary lines of trust that are used to define a committed. Complementary relationships can start off as friendships, but may intensify over time as the feelings of loneliness within the primary intimate relationship increase. These types of risky behaviors become a wrecking ball that can cause the collapse of a committed relationship.

Why Therapy Helps

Intimate partners will experience adverse moments throughout their relationship that create distance. Detachment can derive from a change in employment, the birth of a child, or alterations in daily routines—but couples have to intentionally seek ways to stay connected. Staying connected to your partner is about more than just physically spending time together or exchanging brief descriptions regarding how each other's day went. True connection is about feeling like you are with your partner even when they are miles apart. Couples seek therapy to find ways to develop and sustain connections that are unwavering, even during times of adversity. An unwavering connection between couples is the best way to ward off feelings of loneliness, because both partners are choosing to put each other first. Choosing to put your partner first includes taking the time to assess, plan, implement, and evaluate daily, weekly, or monthly routines that sustain closeness and pre-vent either partner from feeling lonely.

Assessment Phase

In the assessment phase, couples process their individual needs and expectations for how they desire to interact within each other's lives. Often, couples will seek the assistance of a therapist to help them communicate their needs and expectations openly and honestly. The therapist will ask questions that assist each partner with gaining a better understanding about what they desire based on their family of origin and past relationships. Once partners have defined what they need and what they expect from each other, they are then ready to transition to the planning phase.

Planning Phase

During the planning process, couples develop the steps they are willing to take in order to prevent feeling lonely in their relationship. One partner may request that they need uninterrupted time together for a date night once a week to sustain connection. The other partner may ask that they engage in sexual intercourse no less than three times per week in order to feel desired by their partner. The couple will then make arrangements like procuring childcare, altering work schedules, or ensuring they have enough energy to be present in order to attain each other's needs.

In therapy, the couple will process emotional barriers that are not easily talked about, such as feeling neglected when one intimate partner chooses to use their phone as they eat dinner. The couple will use the information gained in therapy to devise plans that prevent these negative feelings from interfering with their connection. Some examples of the systemic changes I have witnessed couples make so they can be more present include leaving their phones in the car or not bringing their laptops when going on vacations. These actions can reduce the potential for distractions and limit the temptations to work instead of focusing on each other. Planning to be present when you are with your partner is a critical part of the preparation process, because it mitigates fore-seeable barriers that can disrupt intimacy. After plans are made, couples then get to implement their agreed-upon actions, which are designed to create unwavering connections.

Implementation Phase

The implementation stage requires that both partners choose to be present and in the moment. This is easier said than done, because life can strike at any moment by subjecting us to a horrible server at a restaurant or an obnoxious moviegoer who happens to be sitting one row behind us in the theater. From therapy, inti-mate partners learn how to deploy mindfulness techniques to assist them with refocusing their attention back onto each other when brief distractions are present. After couples have determined what they want, made their plans, and implemented their agreed-upon action steps, then they are ready to evaluate their progressions toward gaining and sustaining closeness.

Evaluation Phase

The evaluation phase is pivotal for sustaining connection, because partners are able to discuss what they are satisfied with and the areas they need to work on. Both partners may share that they love date night but feel like one time a week is not enough to build the type of connection they are seeking. After comparing schedules, they choose to incorporate a weekly lunch date on Fridays, since their workloads are the lightest that day. In therapy, they are provided with interventions that assist them with being more vulnerable with each other. This in turn allows them to engage in deeper and more meaningful conversations when they take the time to go on dates. The experiences or attempts that partners make to become more connected are all unique, but they compound together and lead couples to feel closer. Unwavering connections are built when partners take these steps to put each other first. The more connected couples feel, the less chances there are for either partner to experience loneliness within the confines of the intimate relationship.

The Four Feelings of Loneliness Within Intimate Relationships

1. ***Isolation*** The unwanted separation from your intimate partner due to the presence of physical barriers that create distance and impede connection.

2. ***Abandonment*** Deserting your intimate partner with-out prefacing your return time or confirming they are secure with your departure.

3. ***Neglect*** Ignoring, forgetting, or overlooking your partner's needs for physical, emotional, social, and recreational intimacy.

4. ***Hopelessness*** The belief that your intimate relationship will not change and the only option left to feel desired again is to end the relationship or pursue a new partner.

Lack of Commitment

Commitments are the agreements that keep relationships together and when couples do not understand why they are in the relation-ship to begin with, they struggle to stay connected. Commitments are often assumed based on relationship titles. But assuming commitment levels based on titles can be dangerous, because titles do not prevent couples from breaching inferred boundaries. Titles alone cannot guarantee each partner will get their relationship needs met unless they are accompanied with defined and agreed-upon roles. Some partners will assume that commitment naturally changes once they get married or have a child, but the only way to truly establish commitment is to have a clear understanding of what each partner desires out of the relationship. Some couples just want to commit to the act of coparenting, which may encompass sharing resources and time in correlation to raising a child. Other couples want the entire life commitment package that comes with the integration of finances, environment, intimacy, and family expansion. Couples who do not understand their partner's thoughts, feelings, needs, and wants have problems establishing and sustaining commitments.

Why Therapy Helps

Kim and Amy, who have been in an undefined cohabitation relationship for one year, entered therapy with issues stemming from commitment. Kim enjoys the relationship for the physical intimacy and companionship. Amy values the shared financial sup-port and equal distribution of domestic responsibilities. They both appreciate the freedom to go on dates with other people and their ability to have open dialogues together without experiencing jealousy. Their relationship took a turn when Amy expressed a desire to have a child either by way of adoption or artificial insemination. Kim is not opposed to having a child with Amy, but feels like they need to establish a clear definition of their commitment prior to entering parenthood. Amy agrees they need to solidify their commitment and is open to the therapeutic intervention of creating a shared relationship agreement that outlines roles, boundaries, needs, wants, and expectations.

After using therapy to process their relationship blueprint, the couple chose to take on the title of "life partners." Their roles and responsibilities as life partners were defined in their relation-ship agreement and included their conjoined relationship principles, bylaws, policies, and procedures. Both partners were a part of developing structure for their relationship based on under-standing and communicating their individual needs, wants, and expectations. Some people may read this example and think it is rigid, and they are right. Committed relationships need to be built on unwavering foundations such as contractual agreements that clearly define how each partner will treat each other. Levinger's Cohesiveness Theory of Commitment and Johnson's Tripartite Typology of Commitment Relationship are two theories that explain the reasons why couples choose to sustain or break their relationship commitments.

Levinger's Cohesiveness Theory of Commitment suggests that intimate partners are compelled to sustain or dissolve relation-ship commitments based on the strength of attraction forces and barrier forces. Attraction forces are pressures that either support the sustainment of the relationship or forces that pull the relation-ship apart. Barrier forces are influences that prevent or make it harder for couples to break their relationship commitment. Some examples are outlined below.

Present Attractions The influential factors that motivate couples to sustain the relationship are considered present attractions. Present attractions satisfy intimate partner's needs of feeling loved, financially secure, and cared for. These types of attractions promote relationship commitment because they meet basic relationship and human needs and wants.

Alternative Attractions The influential factors that pull couples apart or make them consider options outside of sustaining their current relationship are considered alternative attractions. Examples of alternative attractions include other dating prospects, the desire to be single, or the drive to focus solely on professional achievements. These factors are more prevalent in relationships where a stressed or weakened commitment level is already present.

Internal Barriers Intimate partners who feel bound or obligated to sustain their relationship commitment because of religious or cultural beliefs are influenced by internal barriers. Couples with children may feel subjected to the internal barrier of feeling like they failed as parents if they dissolve the relationship. These types of barriers stem from beliefs that are strong enough to override the need for relationship satisfaction and instead view relationship commitments as a requirement.

External Barriers External forces that delays or puts pressure on the couple to sustain the relationship commitment are defined as external barriers. Examples of these barriers include separation and divorce laws that require partners to wait a certain period of time prior to completely dissolving the relationship. Other types of external barriers include family members or friends who might strongly suggest the couple try to repair the relationship instead of ending it.

Johnson's Tripartite Typology of Commitment differs from the basic commitment theories in that it provides a multi-dimensional perspective as to why couples choose to sustain or break relationship commitments. Johnson depicts three separate forms of commitment types which are personal, moral, and structural.

The Four Basic Components of Personal Commitments

Attraction to a Partner The force that compels someone to want to spend time with their partner because they receive physical or emotional gratification from being near them.

Attraction to a Relationship The force that keeps someone attached to the relationship because the union is meeting a goal that would no longer be met if the relationship were to end. These relationship goals are commonly associated with the sustainment of security, comfort, or convenience.

Attraction to Self While in the Relationship The positive feelings and emotions partners develop about themselves while they are in the relationship. Partners may develop an increase in self-confidence or self-worth that they fear they may lose if the relationship were to end.

Relationship Identity Intimate partners who rely on the relationship to define their identity and feel that, if the relationship were to dissolve, they would no longer have value or a purpose in life.

The Four Basic Components of Moral Commitments

Sense of Spiritual or Religious Obligation Partners who choose to stay in the relationship due to feeling that they will go to hell or their soul will be condemned if they divorce.

Sense of Personal Obligation Someone who stays in the relationship based on feeling morally indebted to their partner. This could be a partner who caused pain to their significant other earlier in the relationship and never forgave themselves, so they view the sustainment of the relationship as their personal vindication for past transgressions.

Sense of Consistency with General Values Partners who choose to sustain the commitment because they feel that dissolving the relationship would go against their value system of never quit-ting anything despite how hard or painful it gets.

Sense of Consistency with Specific Beliefs Partners who believe you only get one lifetime opportunity to commit and view their values as nonrefundable, despite the evolution of circumstances and situations.

The Four Basic Components of Structural Commitments

Potential alternatives to the current relationship Will ending the relationship provide me with a lesser, greater, or equal amount of satisfaction?

Perceived social pressure to remain with a current partner How will I be viewed by my family, friends, coworkers, and community if I decide to end the relationship?

Irretrievable investments accrued over the course of a relationship How much time, money, and social capital will I feel like I wasted or lost if the relationship was to end, and can I live in peace knowing I can't get these investments back?

The perceived difficulty of terminating the relationship Will it cost me more to end the relationship or cost me less to learn how to be content with in the relationship?

Reduction in Relationship Satisfaction

Relationship satisfaction is defined by how each partner positively experiences the intimate relationship based on feelings of happiness, fulfilment, support, and enjoyment. Sustaining good feelings for the relationship is easy for couples who are satisfied, because they also experience a greater level of fulfillment. Partners who are fulfilled in their relationship get their needs, wants, and expectations met consistently. In order for couples to sustain satisfaction, they have to be willing to support the attainment of their partner's desires through the relationship. Support comes from expending resources such as time, personal talents, and attention. Couples who are able to experience happiness, fulfilment, and support tend to enjoy the relationship and want to reciprocate the same positive feelings back and forth. Knowledge and understanding are the two keys needed to produce a healthy relationship cycle that yields relationship satisfaction. In order to satisfy an intimate partner, one must first have the knowledge and information regarding what they need, want, and expect. This information should be continually obtained via daily interactions, conversations, and shared experiences, because when couples stop learning about each other then their relationship starts to die.

Why Therapy Helps

Brad and Monica have been in a committed relationship for ten years. Brad works a high-stress job that requires a lot of focus when it comes to speaking and engaging with clients all day. By the time Brad comes home from work, he wants to de-stress by sitting in front of the television watching sports while browsing through social media on his phone. Brad isn't aware of Monica's desire to engage verbally, and she fears addressing her need to communicate because the last time she approached Brad she felt rejected. For several years, Brad has been unaware that Monica has felt like her primary need for engaging in meaningful verbal dialogue has been ignored. While in therapy, Monica had the courage to ask Brad why he doesn't like talking to her. Brad responded by telling Monica he thought she wanted space, so when he comes home every day he just tries to stay out of her way. Brad then shared that he would actually prefer to talk to her daily, but was waiting for her to engage with him. Monica then asked Brad why he was waiting on her and what stopped him from initiating the conversation. Brad said that he had attempted to engage in the past, but felt rejected by the lack of Monica's eye contact when he comes home because she does not look up from her cell phone. Monica shared that she felt the same way.

Monica and Brad used therapy to establish new relationship routines, rituals, and guidelines. They both agreed that when they come home, the first thing they will do is make contact via a hug or kiss. They then requested that they each take mutual responsibility for asking each other deep and meaningful questions about their day. They agreed that their questions should include inquiries about their feelings and how they can please each other. From attending therapy, Brad and Monica were able to gain a better understanding about what they both desired and needed to feel satisfied in their intimate relationship.

The Four Basic Pillars of Relationship Satisfaction

1. **Opportunities** An event or moment when intimate partners can demonstrate the desire to meet each other's needs and wants, without expecting anything in return.

2. **Risks** When couples choose to be vulnerable by requesting their intimate partner meet a specific need or want that can be linked to improving relationship satisfaction.

3. **Rewards** The feelings of happiness, fulfillment, support, and enjoyment that couples experience when they meet each other's needs and sustain high levels of relationship satisfaction.

4. **Costs** The expenditure of energy to learn what your partner needs and the sacrifice of resources such as time, patience, and money in order to meet your inti-mate partner's expectations consistently.

Parenting Issues

Parenting is one the hardest jobs couples encounter because of the many factors that create opportunities for misunderstandings and disagreements. In this section, I will break down three basic approaches that couples learn from therapy in order to mitigate these challenges.

Devising a Team Approach Parents learn quickly that every child has their own set of needs that change throughout their child's stages of development. In order to prevent and reduce the likelihood for misunderstandings, parents have to learn how to work in agreement to establish approaches that consistently meet their child's physical, emotional, and mental needs. Parents who understand their own individual strengths and weaknesses are better at meeting their child's needs. These couples work smarter and not harder by delegating parenting roles and responsibilities based on their individual strengths and weaknesses. In return, these couples experience less stress and sustain deeper emotional connections while parenting together.

Why Therapy Helps

Donna and Ron entered therapy to gain a better understanding for how to parent their adopted child who was born with moderate health defects. During therapy, Donna identified her strengths as being patient, caring, and empathetic. She attached these traits to being raised in a loving household with two overly affectionate parents. Donna's nurturing instincts and her family of origin influenced the couple to agree that she would be primarily responsible for activities associated with their son's meal preparation and medication management. Ron was raised by a single-parent father and was taught to work hard, not make excuses, and value education.

The couple agreed in therapy that based on Ron's upbringing, he would be primarily responsible for implementing discipline strategies, teaching hygiene practices, and managing their son's education. Both Donna and Ron agreed to fulfill responsibilities that over-lapped with their primary roles, but they also felt it would be best to stay in their own parenting lanes as much as possible in order to avoid conflict. During therapy, they processed the importance of remaining in their specific identifiable parenting roles, because that's when they experienced the least amount of misunderstandings.

Managing Individual Parental Blueprints Parents all have an innate parenting blueprint, which derives from how they were raised. This blueprint is implemented consciously and subconsciously based on each partner's level of awareness. When partners know-ingly make a choice to implement or reject a parenting approach, they are referring to their blueprint. Parents use their blueprints to weigh the pros and cons of how an approach impacted them when they were a child and if they will choose to use the same tac-tic or explore an alternative method. Some parents lack awareness and respond instinctively based on transferred emotions that they acquired during childhood. For example, this might be a parent who unknowingly recites phrases that their mother said to them during a triggering moment with their child. These parents are responding subconsciously to their children based on their parental blueprint. Couples who do not first process their own parental blueprint and then share this information with each other might have misunder-standings around finding agreed-upon parenting strategies.

Why Therapy Helps

Landon and Lindsey sought out therapy after having trouble identifying an agreed-upon approach for handling their three-year-old daughter's tantrums. Therapy highlighted that each partner was instinctively implementing the methods they learned from their own parents. Landon responded to his daughter with threats of physical punishment and yelling. Landon remembered how scared he was of his father and attempted to evoke the same fear response in his daughter, thinking that would prevent her from throwing tantrums. His threats did not render the same results and his daughter started to yell even louder when he tried to aggressively change her behavior. Lindsey shared in session how her parents would provide her space to have a tantrum by ignoring her. She stated that they had a lot of patience and never yelled or screamed. Lindsey tried this same approach with her daughter, but couldn't handle the embarrassment of seeing her daughter roll on the ground in public. After less than a minute of trying to be patient she would appease her daughter's desire in an attempt to end the tantrum.

In therapy, the couple was provided information explaining why children respond differently based on their current stage of development. The two developmental phases that are commonly noted by parents as being the most difficult are the toddler and teenage years. Landon and Lindsey were influenced by the infor-mation they gained in therapy and took the time between sessions to learn more about their daughter's current stage of development. They also gained more insight on how their parental blueprints were established and what they could do to develop mutually agreed-upon partnering strategies. Both of these partners imple-mented actions that derive from their blueprints, which are based on their past interactions with their parents. The couple learned in therapy that their blueprints can evolve by educating themselves on parenting methods that align with their child's stages of devel-opment. Therapy helps couples add to their parenting blueprints by assisting them with processing their own childhood experiences and helping them identify scholarly information that can be used to make edits to their current parental blueprint.

Filtering Out External Factors Media outlets, friends, and relatives all provide information on wrong and right ways to parent. Couples need to choose carefully who and what they listen to when it pertains to influencing their parenting. Most importantly, they need to learn how to listen and understand each other. Couples will experience relationship problems if they allow the influences of external factors to have a greater voice in their relationship than each other. This is especially true when related to decisions they make involving their children. Partners are less inclined to trust each other when they do not feel like their voices are heard. This is why referencing parenting advice from another parent, family member, or friend over the suggestions given by your intimate partner can create problems.

Why Therapy Helps

Erica and Manny come from two different family environments and expose themselves to media outlets that support opposing views. Erica believes in the conservation of resources—saving money and making do with what you already have. Manny was raised in a privileged family that allowed him to travel the world, gain access to life's finest luxuries, and receive things freely. Erica listens to religious-based media outlets that reinforce her conser-vative views and Manny exposes himself to more liberal speakers, who describe abundance as a natural birthright. The couple finds themselves constantly fighting about the amount of money they spend on their son's clothes, education, and entertainment.

While in therapy the couple was afforded a safe space to express their individual beliefs and, in turn, they developed a stronger bond of trust which was bred through understanding each other's viewpoints. Prior to therapy, Manny believed their son should wear only name-brand clothes, attend private schools, and be given any device or toy he requested. Erica did not understand why their son could not wear cheaper store-brand clothing, attend public schools, and pay for his toys with money he earned from doing chores. In ther-apy, the couple worked to understand each other by taking the time to process their individual viewpoints, without the external distrac-tions brought on by their chosen media outlets.

In the first session, Manny shared his belief that name-brand items hold up better during the washing process, which prevents the frequency of buying clothing as often. Erica affirmed Manny's viewpoint that quality clothing does last longer, but noted the sav-ings were lost because their son's rapid growth spurts meant hav-ing to purchase clothing more often—regardless of the quality. Manny was able to agree with his wife's assessment and shared that he understood why she felt like purchasing new clothes for every event could feel like a wasted expense. The couple agreed to only buy name-brand outfits for church, family events, and picture days. They decided to dress their son in less expensive clothing for activities such as lounging around the house, playing outside with friends, and night wear. From effectively listening to each other, the couple was able to quickly gain a better understanding of the other's perspective.

As therapy progressed, they moved on to processing the topic of education, but this time the therapist was less involved in direct-ing the dialogue . This was done so that the couple could have the space they needed to sharpen their newfound comprehension skills as they worked to develop more effective behavioral patterns. Manny started by sharing that he believed a private school envi-ronment would provide their son with a better education and less of a chance that he'd be bullied at school. Erica responded by noting the fact that they had specifically purchased their home in a neighborhood that was zoned to the top school district in the state based on high testing scores, a high percentage of board-certified teachers, and a low number of student disciplinary incidences—and that, by placing their son in private school, they weren't utilizing these benefits. Manny thanked his wife for that reminder and shared how he had forgotten about those factors as a big reason for why they had bought their home. Erica affirmed Manny's desire to provide their son with a sound and safe learning environment. The couple then developed an agreement that entailed sending their son to the local public school while investing additional resources in private tutoring, summer camps, and extracurricular activities outside of school.

During the closing phase of therapy, the clinician directed the couple to use the same comprehension techniques they learned in therapy at home between sessions, to process the topic of large purchases and gifts. Erica was able to effectively express to Manny that she feared their son would grow up spoiled and entitled. Manny validated her feelings and shared how he felt social pres-sures to provide his son the same luxuries he was given as a child. After the couple heard each other's feelings, they agreed to imple-ment a reward system that allowed their son the ability to receive gifts based on how well he performed at school and at home. They chose to award their son gifts when he completed small chores and did well in school, so he would learn how to earn things based on his behaviors. Therapy assisted the couple by giving them the space to block out external influences. Once they eliminated out-side voices, they were able to focus on the views and options that truly mattered the most—their own. Manny and Erica took the time to process and understand each other's individual beliefs, and developed agreed-upon parenting guidelines that aligned with what they both felt would be best for their son.

The Four Parenting Styles

Authoritative This parenting style is ideal for couples who strive to find the right balance between demanding and responsive par-enting approaches. Authoritative parents are known to be chil-dren-centered, which is defined by their ability to set clear standards, implement supportive disciplinary methods, and demonstrate high levels of parental involvement. These parents also tend to be bet-ter communicators, more encouraging, and strive to empower their children to be independent and self-sufficient.

Authoritarian This parenting style is most commonly imple-mented by individuals who associate with lower social economical statuses, less education, and were raised by strict and judgmental caretakers themselves. Authoritative parents are dictators who do not trust their kids, enforce harsh punishments, and believe chil-dren should be seen and not heard. These parents exhibit little patience, are control-centered, and do not communicate well.

Indulgent This parenting style is also known as "permissive," because indulgent parents are very lenient and avoid conflict at all costs. Permissive parents can come from both privileged and adverse settings, attempting to overcompensate for having overly lenient or restrictive parents, and subconsciously emulate their own parents' passive parental behaviors. These parents either fear or do not know how to establish appropriate parent-child bound-aries, attempt to see their children as friends, and make excuses for their child's negative behaviors.

Uninvolved This parenting style can also be classified as neglect-ful, because uninvolved parents are neither responsive nor demand-ing. These parents may suffer from mental illnesses that limit empathic, caring, and nurturing responses or they have abusive, neglectful, and traumatic histories which prevent them from raising healthy children. Uninvolved parenting sits on the spectrum of abuse, because they fail to meet their children's basic needs.

Barriers that Block Intimate Partners from Feeling Understood

Each partner is required at all times to govern the attainment of their relationship needs, wants, and expectations. This process starts during the planning phase that occurs prior to developing a committed intimate relationship. This pre-relationship phase is also called the courtship or "talking" phase, in which both partners are assessing each other's potential as long-term mates. In order for understanding to flow freely, couples have to dispel any false beliefs or expectations during this phase. This requires couples to slow down the euphoric feelings that commonly occur during the honeymoon period. When couples are riding the bliss of new-ness, they have to remember to peel back the layers of what they both need, want, and expect from each other and a relationship together.

Partners who fail to ask specific questions and hold their pro-spective mate accountable for their current routines, habits, and behaviors will result in attempting to guess at what their partner is feeling—referred to in therapy as "mind reading." When there is not a definitive answer present, our brains will fill in the gap with what we want to hear or see. In a relationship that involves infi-delity at the onset, this could manifest as telling yourself that your prospective partner will be faithful to you once they leave their other relationship—despite your never asking them if they intend on growing a future with you or if they are just using you as a tem-porary placeholder until they decide to recommit with their cur-rent partner. This example of mind reading will influence you to blame your prospective partner for hurting you. Blame is a result of displacing emotions into a space that prevents you from hav-ing to be accountable for them. You will blame someone else for causing you pain or making you angry without first assessing the role you played in creating the current outcome. Understanding is blocked between intimate partners when they create anony-mous expectations, attempt to read each other's minds, blame one another for their individual situations, and allow their emotions to master their decisions.

- Anonymous Expectations
- Mind Reading
- Blaming
- Emotions

Anonymous Expectations

Prior to establishing a romantic relationship, it is important to know what you expect from yourself, your intimate partner, and the relationship as a whole. Our expectations are birthed from the hopes, beliefs, and desired outcomes that we anticipate manifesting in ourselves, our intimate partner, and our relationship. Expectations produce misunderstandings between intimate partners when they are not verbalized or directly communicated.

As the master of yourself, you are expected to identify, communicate, and obtain what you need to live your best life. No one is responsible for your happiness besides you. You will always be expected to govern your own self-development, self-discipline, and self-worth externally from any relationship you develop. When I encounter a partner during couples therapy who states they do not know what they want from their life, I immediately recommend they pursue individual therapy, life coaching, or seek some form of spiritual guidance to find answers to what they want. Before attempting to build an intimate relationship with another person, it is essential to first understand what you are willing to give and what you expect to receive in return. Couples who build relationships on a foundation of anonymous expectations will develop problems with understanding each other as the relationship progresses. Highlighting what you need, want, and expect from your intimate partner is required in order for genuine understanding to exist.

You should always expect your intimate partner to conduct themselves in a manner that enables you to feel safe, heard, under-stood, and cared for within the relationship. In order to hold your partner accountable for these expectations, you have to provide them with responses that teach them how to treat you. My favorite example of this involves a personal story. During the first big fight my wife and I experienced while we were dating in college, she abruptly hung up the phone on me in the middle of a heated verbal exchange. I paused, and then called her back. When she picked up the phone, I told her with a calm voice that we were building a relationship and we should both expect that there will be times when we will make each other upset, but we have to maintain a mutual level of respect. I then asked her to request space when she starts to feel overwhelmed, instead of hanging up the phone or leaving without warning. I also promised her I would honor her request for space without attempting to continue the dialogue or hold her hostage. We have used this technique over the course of our relationship, and it has helped us build trust because we never established bad habits such as hanging up the phone or abruptly abandoning each other during moments of conflict. Instead, we tell each other what we need and trust that the other one will honor the request without hesitation. At the beginning of the relationship, this was very hard because I like to solve issues immediately. Over time, I gained a better understanding for her need to process her own thoughts, feelings, and emotions independently, prior to re-engaging with me. My wife developed an understanding for my need to know a time for us to reconvene later, so I do not have to anxiously wonder when or if we will work through the issue. She always honors her time frame, which allows me to willingly and consistently give her space when she asks.

Both partners need to enter the relationship expecting it to serve as a booster or conductor for their current emotions and feelings. I tell partners that if you were not happy with yourself or life prior to the relationship, chances are you could end up reducing the happiness of your prospective partner, or you could attract someone who is also miserable and you will be unhappy together. Two negative people or one positive and one negative person both equal a negative relationship. You should expect the relationship to be the magnifier of whatever emotions and behaviors with which each partner enters the relationship. If your partner has a history of being untrustworthy, selfish, or abusive, then they will bring the same behaviors into a new relationship. These behaviors will follow them unless they choose to do the hard work on themselves to correct their negative behaviors. Relationships yield a return based on what each partner brings to the table.

The hardest part of my job as a relationship therapist is providing nonbiased counsel to couples who do not like each other but over time have developed feelings that keep them attached. This happens when one or both partners were happier by themselves or prior to the relationship, but they now have binding attachments such as kids or finances that force them to attempt to make the relationship work. To avoid becoming attached to someone you will dislike later, select an intimate partner who is content with what you want to offer in a relationship and someone who agrees with your expectations.

Why Therapy Helps

Talk therapy is a series of strategic conversations designed to alter habits and create sustainable behavior changes within individuals and systems. The process is governed by outcomes that align with the attainment of specific, measurable, realistic, and timely goals. Therapy assists couples with establishing their expectations because the therapeutic process mirrors the success or failure of specific outcomes being met. This is why therapy always works regardless of whether the goals are obtained or not. Couples always leave therapy with an understanding of their partner's desire to take the necessary steps for change to occur. If an intimate partner refuses to apply the interventions or do the assigned work in therapy, then they are communicating via their actions that they do not expect or want to change. People decide to change only when change becomes easier than remaining the same. The partner who chooses not to apply the relationship counseling is then choosing to remain the same. Couples who do apply the therapeutic approaches and see a benefit still may not sustain their goals if they expect the rewards to be maintained without continuous effort. Relationships are ongoing and therapy assists couples by illustrating the amount of work that is required not only to repair a relationship but also to sustain it. From the process of counseling, one or both partners may find they desire a different set of expectations for themselves or from their partner in order to receive the relationship satisfaction they are both seeking.

The Four T's for Relationship Expectations

Trustworthiness Expect to feel secure that your partner will behave in a desirable manner in your presence and absence based on a mutually agreed-upon code of relationship conduct.

Thoughtfulness Expect your partner to demonstrate a mutual sense of care and desire to fulfill your needs and wants by adding to the positive feelings and emotions you both brought into the relationship during the conception or honeymoon stage.

Thankfulness Expect to feel valued and appreciated by your partner for the things you do, the words you speak, and the devotion you demonstrate consistently to enhance the quality of their life daily.

Togetherness Expect to combine your good fortune, experiences, decision-making power, and resources in order to produce a greater outcome for your lives that could not be possible independently of the relationship.

Mind Reading

As intimate partners grow their relationship, they establish a collection of memories and experiences that range in satisfaction. Couples will start to expect their partner to duplicate gratifying memories and avoid the unsatisfying experiences. Couples will establish these two expectations, despite the absence of a shared understanding taking place through dialogue and processing. These couples, in turn, are expecting their partners to read their minds.

Mind reading is one of the greatest barriers that prevents understanding, because partners are expecting their significant other to know how to respond in every situation. Our intimate partners have a harder time accurately responding the way we want them to, unless they are first given specific standards that outline our expectations, needs, and wants. Mind reading takes place when couples assume their partner will respond the same way based on a previous experience. We cannot expect our partner to know what we are thinking, feeling, or needing, despite how close we become. Furthermore, we cannot assume that our partner will respond the same way as they did in the past because we are all constantly changing and evolving.

When Kenny and Lesley first started dating, Kenny was the owner of several rental properties that he leased out to families in order to produce a stream of sustainable cash flow. Over time, Kenny's ability to be his own boss inspired Lesley to quit her job as an art teacher. Lesley used her art experience and degree in marketing to open a clothing store. Lesley thought that Kenny would embrace her as a fellow entrepreneur, but as her store became more successful, she began to notice an increase in arguments. The couple's fighting began to increase and hit a peak during one heated exchange when Kenny voiced the concern that he felt like Lesley was trying to emasculate him. Kenny went on to explain that he felt like he had more value in the relationship when he was earning the majority of the money. He shared that his sense of value came from financially supporting Lesley so she could impact the world through teaching. Lesley responded that she assumed Kenny viewed her as weak because she was reliant on a job for money instead of her own ability to generate revenue. She continued by sharing that her intention of joining him as a business owner was to bring them closer because they would have more in common. Lesley then asked Kenny why it took him so long to say something. He responded by saying, "In my mind, I thought you would start to realize how I felt since we started arguing more." Mind reading lead this couple to go years without gaining the proper understanding for how they both felt.

Why Therapy Helps

Lesley and Kenny entered therapy with an extensive history of failed mind readings. They were both wrong when it came to guessing what the other was thinking, and their inaccuracy with predicting each other's thoughts influenced their heated fights. Couples therapy immediately helped by slowing them down so they both could be heard. They were instructed during the first session to assign speaker and receiver roles when discussing emotionally charged topics. The speaker was challenged with the role of transmitting their verbal messages in small tangents that lasted no longer than ten seconds. This was done to permit too much information from being sent at one time. The receiver was responsible for reciting back only what they heard their partner say, with-out interjecting their own words, thoughts, or feelings. When partners practice active listening, they need only repeat the words they hear their significant other saying in order to prevent misunderstandings and defensiveness. Once the messages are transmitted, the receiver then gets to ask the sender questions that are designed to gain a better understanding for why and how they feel the way they do.

For example, when Lesley was operating as the sender and Kenny was in the role of receiver, he asked Lesley to tell him more about why she did not like him hanging out with his friend Steve. Lesley shared that she felt like Kenny envied Steve's bachelor life and that he was a bad influence on their marriage because he constantly hooked up with different women he met online. Kenny responded by reciting back what he heard Lesley say. He then debunked Lesley's failed attempt at reading his mind by validating he was completely happy with their monogamous relation-ship. Kenny further shared that his friend Steve actually envied him because he was able to find and sustain a secure relationship with Lesley. The couple was able to use therapy to slow down their dialogues so their attempts at mindreading could be discredited before heated arguments ensued. Therapy helps couples gain and process accurate information, so they do not have to rely on their hypotheses, which are based in failed mind reading attempts.

The Four Phrases of Mind Reading

1. ***"In my mind I thought it was going to be . . ."*** Couples who form conclusions in their own heads and fail to account for alternative outcomes.

2. ***"What I thought you would have done is . . ."*** Couples predicting how their partner will act based on what they conceptualized to be the ideal or desired response.

3. ***"I know you don't want to, so I went ahead and . . ."*** Couples gaining data from a past experience their partner liked or disliked, and then using that information to make a future decision without consulting one another.

4. ***"Remember when I do that you usually . . ."*** Couples expecting their partner to repeat a past response the same exact way during a future interaction.

Blaming

When mistakes are made, couples first attempt to assign blame instead of seeking understanding. Blame prevents understanding because it creates an emotional response in your partner that makes them want to defend their actions. For partners who don't become defensive, blame might cause them to internalize feelings of shame, guilt, and regret. Both of these responses prevent understanding from occurring because blame shifts the focus to what happened and ignores *why* or *how* it happened.

I want to add that there is a thin line between blaming your partner and holding your partner accountable for their actions. Many of the couples I treat that seek relationship counseling are attempting to heal from some form of hurt or betrayal. The most common occurrence is when one or both partners are unfaithful. The cheated-on partner will blame the other for hurting them but will fail to understand why it happened. Understanding why the betrayal happened will give the hurt partner the information they need to decide if the relationship is worth salvaging, or if they should end the intimate relationship altogether. Understanding is a hard ask, because people often do not want to know the truth. It is easier to simply place blame and remain the victim than to risk learning that you may have contributed or influenced your partner's negative choices. As a couples therapist, I do not see either partner as a victim, and that applies to couples I treat for infidelity as well. I conceptualize infidelity and betrayal cases by processing six factors: relationship, environment, opportunities, circumstances, choices, and actions.

The relationship and the environment are indicative to the level of satisfaction that is present between the couple prior to the betrayal occurring. I find that, in most infidelity cases, one or both partners were experiencing a strained emotional relation-ship within an ungratifying environment that rendered low levels of satisfaction for a long time. These low levels of satisfaction make partners more susceptible to the opportunities and circumstances which influence their choices and actions that demonstrate breeches in trust.

For one husband whom I treated in couples counseling, the environment in which he lived was a fertile breeding ground for infidelity, especially for a man who was miserable in his marriage. The husband worked predominantly around single women and found himself in situations daily where he was receiving emotional validation from women who were not his wife. The interest he was getting from his female coworkers was magnified because he felt unappreciated in his marital relationship and home environment. In therapy, we explored his feelings that, prior to the infidelity, his marriage turned into a business partnership which only encompassed managing kids, income, and household duties. His work environment produced daily opportunities and circumstances to be around women who sought his attention sexually, despite knowing he was married. After seeking validation from his workplace and not his marriage, he gave in to temptations and developed several secondary intimate relationships with his female coworkers, which spiraled into a number of infidelities. His wife learned about one of the many affairs after she caught him sending explicit messages to a woman he worked with.

Oddly enough, I find the majority of partners who get caught cheating feel a mild sense of relief, because they never intended to leave the original relationship for the affair partner. These deceitful partners report feeling like the infidelity was equivalent to being taken off emotional life support and they could feel again. When they get caught it is freeing, because they know a decision now has to be made. Some couples choose to repair themselves and the relationship, and others make the choice to end the marriage or uncommitted relationship.

Despite the relationship, environment, opportunities, and circumstances that presented themselves, partners need to be held accountable for their choices and actions. Infidelity is never justified, because there is always the choice to dissolve or attempt to repair the current relationship prior to engaging with someone outside of the marital or committed union.

Why Therapy Helps

Clients who choose to work on rebuilding their relationship after infidelity are informed of the risks and benefits of treatment at the beginning of the process. The cheating partner is made aware that they are choosing to forfeit some of the freedoms they once had prior to the discovery of the infidelity. The loss of privacy is the biggest freedom that has to be given up by the cheating partner in order for the healing process to start. Privacy has to be given up because it emulates the secrecy that was used to sustain the deception needed to fuel infidelity.

Cheating partners who blame themselves for the loss of freedoms and then provide their betrayed intimate partner with full access to information are choosing to embrace accountability. Choosing to be accountable starts by accepting that your past actions created your current situation. Accountability is important for change, because it is the self-acknowledgment that new actions are required in order to produce a change in the future. The primary action that produces healing for couples coping with infidelity is openness and vulnerability. Couples seek therapy to learn about the actions that are required to gain the results they desire. Without the direction provided by a well-trained couples therapist, intimate partners can resort back to their default settings, which can include unhelpful habits, such as assigning blame. Blame is a wasted action that impedes couples from healing and moving forward in their relationship. Therapy helps by replacing blame with accountability.

The Four Questions that Replace Blame with Accountability

How did this happen? Asking *how* assists partners in identifying and understanding the progressive steps that lead up to the negative decisions or choices that took place within the relationship.

When did this happen? Knowing when and for how long the infidelity took place assists partners with conceptualizing the time-frame and the other events that were taking place while the transgressions were happening.

What roles did we each play? Asking about the roles each partner played assists in determining the amount of accountability (if any) you need in order to accept what happened, and the amount of responsibility your partner needs to accept that they caused the negative event to happen.

Could we have done things differently? Asking if things could have been done differently assists partners both in identify-ing ways to prevent the negative event from occurring again and in determining the probability the event will happen again.

Emotions

The *Oxford English Dictionary* defines an *emotion* as "a strong feeling deriving from one's circumstances, mood, or relationships with others." Emotions can easily block a couple's ability to seek understanding because they originate from strong feelings that produce physio-logical and psychological stimuli. Physiological responses produced by emotions such as fear create fight or flight reactions, which occur when there are increased levels of stress or danger. Psychological stimuli can create racing thoughts, an increase in negative self-talk, or produce a complete mental shutdown that looks like the absence of all thoughts. These physiological and psychological stimuli need time to run their courses before intimate partners can accurately seek to find understanding after experiencing any event that escalates emotions between them. Paul Eckman, a psychologist known best for researching emotions and how they influence facial expressions, defined six basic emotions. I will describe these emotions and provide examples of how they can block understanding. Although there are several other emotions not found on this list, these six emotions will be used as a template to explore how emotions block understanding between intimate partners.

Happiness is the most desired of the six basic emotions, because it correlates with feelings of euphoria, joy, satisfaction, and wholeness. Feelings of happiness are acquired by internal and external sources. Internal characteristics that influence happiness are high levels of self-worth, self-discipline, self-esteem, and self-accomplishments. External factors that contribute to feeling happy come from outside sources, such as people, places, or things. It is ideal to have a blend of both internal and external factors that influence happiness but, within intimate relationships, couples can lose their ability to gain understanding when they become overly reliant on their partner to make them happy. I identify these couples in therapy when one partner continues to get hurt by the other because they have become dependent solely on that person to make them happy.

Roger and Linda sought couples therapy to break a cycle of lying and betrayal that was causing Roger to question the sustainability of the relationship. Roger confessed that he felt like Linda was his greatest source of happiness and that he needed her in his life to feel good about himself. Linda shared that she did not feel the same way about Roger and was in the relationship solely for the financial security he provided. Despite all of Linda's transgressions coming to light, therapy concluded with Linda gaining the freedom to openly sustain relationships with other men simultaneous to remaining in her marriage. Roger chose to enter into an open marriage, sharing his wife emotionally and sexually with other men in order to retain the feelings of happiness he gained from their marriage. In this case, I believe Roger's desire to feel happiness blocked his ability to understand that he was choosing to settle for a wife who confessed that she viewed him as no more than a source of financial stability. I referred both Roger and Linda to seek individual therapy in order to explore how the marriage transformed their belief and value systems. Both declined the recommendation, stating that from couples counseling they identified a solution that makes them both feel happy.

Sadness is an emotion that people experience when they feel disappointed, let down, hopeless, or encounter loss and grief. When sadness lingers, it can morph into depression. The American Psychiatric Association defines depression as "a common and serious medical illness that negatively affects how you feel, the way you think, and how you act." Depressed people will exhibit low levels of energy, lethargic moods, trouble sleeping, thoughts of death, and difficulty concentrating. Feelings of sadness can block understanding between intimate partners by distorting their ability to think clearly and make rational decisions. When one partner is experiencing high levels of sadness or depression, they are more susceptible to relinquishing their decision-making power.

When Donnie experienced the death of his father, he was inclined to follow his wife's lead. This included quitting his job and moving across the country to live closer to her family in North Carolina. Two years after they moved, Donnie and his wife entered couples therapy seeking to find relief, and to process Donnie's pent-up feelings of resentment towards his wife. In therapy, it was revealed that Donnie felt like his wife took advantage of his saddened and depressed state to get what she always wanted, which was to move back home. To make matters worse, Donnie was having a difficult time finding a good job, and blamed his wife for their income struggles and him leaving his dream job to move to North Carolina. This couple ultimately chose to end the relation-ship because Donnie was unable to regain the trust in their relationship. He felt like his wife had taken advantage of his saddened emotional state, and ultimately couldn't forgive her.

Disgust is similar to the other emotions, in that it stems from an activating stimulus, but differs in the fact that the stimulus is directly associated to an undesirable sight, smell, or sound. Disgust produces feelings of repulsion and physical illness, and creates a natural desire to withdraw from the source that is causing the per-son to feel disgusted. Disgust blocks understanding from occurring between couples because it is a great distraction that inhibits communication. As I defined in earlier sections, communication is the transmission of messages being sent and received. Communication becomes strained if a couple cannot stand to continue the communication sequence due to feelings of disgust.

While working with a couple named Dianne and Eric, who came to therapy to treat infidelity, Dianne became nauseous when hearing the name of Eric's affair partner. The name of Eric's affair partner triggered feelings of disgust in Dianne that were so strong she would literally experience a gag reflex when hearing the name in session. Dianne's feelings of disgust grew even stronger after she found a pair of the woman's underwear in Eric's gym bag, which he retained as a keepsake after he ended the affair. In order for the couple to proceed through therapy without producing feelings of disgust in Dianne, we had to develop an alternate name when referencing Eric's affair partner. After almost a full year in therapy, the couple was able to heal from the infidelity—but, Dianne con-fessed, she will never be able to hear the name of the affair partner again without feeling like she has to vomit.

Fear is an emotion that is often misunderstood because of the physiological response that occurs when people become frightened. Fear activates the adrenal glands to release cortisol into the bloodstream, triggering a fight-or-flight response. Cortisol levels increase our blood pressure, delay insulin uptake inhibitors, and speed up our heart rates. These responses are vital in supporting the increased flow of blood to our larger muscle groups, so we can be equipped with extra energy to ward off or flee threats and danger. When we sustain high levels of cortisol over long periods of time, it can be harmful to our body, mind, and relationships. Fear threatens our relationships because, when we become scared, our sensitivity to danger is heightened and this blocks our ability to process information. When couples experience relationship traumas such as breaches in trust or betrayals, partners will fear being hurt again. The fear that your partner will hurt you again can create a relationship environment rife with high levels of anxiety and paranoia. These high levels of cortisol in the bloodstream make it hard for a hurt partner to find understanding.

Anger is similar to fear because it activates the same chemical reactions that create a fight-or-flight response. Like fear, anger is viewed by most as a negative emotion that people struggle to manage. When anger is managed effectively, it can be used as a tool that gives us insight into something that we feel is wrong. Anger is typically the first emotion that is activated when we feel like our intimate partner is not treating us with respect, equality, or appreciation. In therapy, one can expect to witness anger on display in some fashion after a couple experiences hurt. When both partners are angry, understanding is usually blocked by violence, aggression, disrespect, or abuse. It is challenging, if not impossible, for two angry intimate partners to sit down alone with each other and display the empathic listening required to fully understand what happened, nonetheless develop a plan to heal from it. This is because anger is a flooding emotion that produces high intense levels of expression with little or no warning. The phrase "going from zero to one hundred" is accurate in representing how quickly couples can transition from calm to explosive when attempting to have a dialogue around content that produces feelings of anger. Even experienced couples therapists will find it challenging not to unintentionally set off emotional landmines in sessions with couples that are experiencing heightened forms of anger.

While in session with Caleb and Sasha, anger erupted without any warning and blocked their ability to gain understanding around the primary reason they sought therapy. In an attempt to assist Caleb in gaining a better understanding for why Sasha criticizes him for not sustaining employment, we began to process Sasha's relationship with her father. Our goal was to help Caleb understand how Sasha's family of origin triggers her to feel unsafe when he is not working. Sasha's dad worked the same job for thirty-five years prior to retiring. Sasha had stated in past sessions that she honors her father for his sacrifice to work around the clock so her mother could be a homemaker. As we were developing the connection between Sasha's dad and how her need for Caleb to sustain employment aligned with her emotional safety, Caleb abruptly made a statement that instantly set Sasha off. Caleb said to Sasha, "I don't want to be like your father who worked the same job for thirty-five years while abandoning you and your mother." Caleb's comments provoked anger in Sasha, and she fired back at Caleb by saying, "My father is a real man who took care of his family and kept a job, something you aren't able to do." The couple began to throw verbal jabs back and forth, ignoring my attempts to regain control of the session. I ended up having to separate the couple and, once their anger temporarily subsided, we were able to continue therapy. As we proceeded with therapy, Sasha stated that she didn't understand how Caleb could so easily push her buttons, driving her from zero to one hundred so fast. I informed both partners that anger is an emotion that can be easily triggered by those who are the closest to us. This is why it is so easy for intimate partners to become angry with each other. The closer someone is to you, the more they know, and their knowledge about you (or apparent lack thereof) becomes a source of anger. In the case of this couple, Caleb had developed a pattern where he would use knowledge about Sasha to ignite anger. We knew his actions were intentional because, when he made Sasha angry, she easily became distracted and stopped holding him accountable for not sustaining employment. As we progressed through therapy, I highlighted the couple's cycle of conflict and helped them see how anger blocked their ability to gain understanding and enforce accountability.

Surprise is the reaction brought on by some form of unexpected or unanticipated action. Despite the type of surprise, be it good or bad, this emotion can have the same result—a moment of feeling shocked, startled, or stunned. When couples experience surprise, they can be thrown off-kilter and lose their ability to understand each other. I see this often in therapy when one partner reveals information that is surprising. Eli and Beth were dating for fifteen years and had five children together during their time as cohabitating unmarried partners. Eventually, they initiated premarital therapy to resolve past trauma stemming from infidelity and abandonment issues. I worked with them over the course of eight months, leading up to the week before their wedding day. During our final session, Eli revealed he no longer felt connected to Beth and he wanted to dissolve the relationship. Beth and I were both surprised, but since I was not emotionally connected to the relationship, I was able to try to seek understanding. As we attempted to gain more insight on Eli's feelings, Beth began to yell, curse, scream, and shout at Eli. She started to talk about how their wed-ding was in seven days—how she spent so much money on her dress, the venue, and food. More importantly, Beth shared how she would look like a fool when telling her family and friends the wed-ding had been canceled. Beth's first emotion was surprise, which stemmed from her hearing Eli say he didn't want to get married anymore. After the initial shock, Beth was then flooded with rage that was so powerful it caused her to leave the session without understanding why Eli felt like they needed to cancel the wedding. Beth's feelings disabled the discovery process and blocked her from further understanding. The couple chose not to continue therapy, so we never got to process Eli's feelings or treat the shock he produced in Beth with his remarks.

Why Therapy Helps

When I was an undergraduate student working as an intern for a behavior modification program, I was introduced to the quote, "emotions are poor masters but great servants." Since then, I have applied this message to my own life and the clients I treat in therapy. Gaining more insight into your feelings and emotions so they do not master your decisions is a key benefit that is received from therapy. Therapy assists individuals and couples with identifying, understanding, and using their emotions. Emotions are powerful influencers that have the potential to strip away our ability to govern our actions. Therapy helps couples use their emotions to get what they need, want, and desire out of life and their intimate relationships. Clients are taught in therapy how to use their emotions to serve them. Couples therapists assess the current emotions that are present within both partners, and then they use selected interventions to help each partner communicate their feelings in constructive ways. Negative emotions are the hardest feelings that couples struggle to manage, because they come from past or current events in their relationship. When negative feelings are stored up, they will start to erode the relationship connection. Prior to attending therapy, couples will try to process their feelings together, but may get caught in the story. The story is the tip of the iceberg that sits atop the deep-rooted emotions that make up the narrative. Well-trained therapists have the ability to surgically remove emotions from any storyline while tracking the facts sur-rounding what happened. Once the emotions are extracted, the therapist helps the couple use them to evoke sustainable behavior changes. Change is produced from the paradigm shift that occurs after couples learn how their actions generate specific emotional responses in their partner. After each partner gains an understanding of how their words or actions shaped certain emotional responses in their partner, only then can couples start the healing process. Understanding allows partners to display empathy, which is an important ingredient in helping couples use their emotions to repair, rather than hinder, their relationship.

The Four Emotional Responses that Block Understanding

Disrespect Actions and words that hurt your intimate partner by making them feel belittled, insulted, or ignored.

Shutdown A human safety response in which all communication with your partner is disabled until your emotions go back to homeostasis, or until your partner's repair attempt is received.

Aggression Verbal and physical assaults that are hostile in nature because they threaten feelings of safety and security.

Abandonment Abruptly leaving or walking out on your partner without first establishing your need to briefly take some space.

Chapter 4

REASON 4: TO FEEL CARED FOR

"I want you, and I want you to want me too." This verse comes from a song by my favorite jazz singer Sade. I often recite this line in therapy with couples when introducing the topic of feeling cared for by your intimate partner. Feeling cared for by another person is a human need, and is the corner-stone of all deep and meaningful relationships. How is feeling cared for by our intimate partner measured or quantified? I often turn to Gary Chapman's book *The 5 Love Languages* to answer this question, because he defines five basic ways couples demonstrate their desire and care for each other. Dr. Chapman introduces five basic actions as "love languages" and suggests we all have a primary love language. Before diving deeper and exploring these love languages, I would like to provide a brief disclaimer. When con-ducting therapy with couples, I intentionally refrain from using the word "love." Love, for most people, is associated with a *feeling*—but love should be defined as a verb or action word. We show our love through the actions we display, which makes love less about how we feel (or say we feel) and more about how we demonstrate that feeling. Dr. Chapman defined these five choices in his book as ways to demonstrate the love we have for our intimate partners.

The Five Love Actions Based on the Five Love Languages

- Initiating physical contact
- Reciting words of affirmation
- Planning and engaging in quality time together
- Delivering gifts or tangible sentiments
- Performing acts of service

Physical Contact

As a trained and licensed marriage and family therapist, one of the first therapeutic interventions I conduct with all new clients is the illustration of their "genogram." The concept of genograms originated from Murray Bowen, who was a renowned psychiatrist and a major contributor to the field of marriage and family therapy. Genograms map out our family of origin across a minimum of three generations, and illustrate demographics such as gender, age, occupation, socioeconomic statutes, mental and physical health history, and past traumas. Genograms also explore the attachments and cutoffs between different family members. While processing clients' genograms, I also inquire about how each partner experienced feeling cared for by their parents and caretakers. Clients who express feeling cared for through touch can trace the origin of this need to childhood experiences of receiving unlimited amounts of physical contact, or their desire for these experiences without ever having them met.

These two ends of the touch spectrum are correlating factors that define a partner's current desire or lack of desire for physical touch. Although the statement "opposites attract" is true when applied to several other relationship characteristics, physical con-tact is usually not applicable. I recall a session, working with a couple named Antonio and Sherly, who had different expectations pertaining to the amount, frequency, and type of physical contact they each desired in order to feel cared for. Antonio only wanted physical contact during the act of sex, but Sherly desired some form of touch whenever she was in Antonio's presence. Sherly felt like Antonio was ashamed of her or embarrassed to be with her in public because he would reject her hand when she reached out to hold his, or he would turn his head when she leaned in for a kiss. Sherly later learned in couples therapy that Antonio was abused as a child by a female caretaker and viewed all forms of physical touch as relinquishing some control over his body. As we went deeper in therapy and explored Antonio's intimate relationship history with previous partners, we also learned that Antonio relied heavily on alcohol and drugs in order to feel comfortable enough to be physically intimate. We then linked the couple's decrease in physical intimacy to around the time Antonio got sober from sub-stances and returned home from inpatient treatment. Antonio did not originally desire physical contact because he viewed touch as unsafe. From couples therapy, Sherly learned how to assist Antonio by reintroducing him to intimate touch in a way that was safe and enjoyable for them both.

Words of Affirmation

One of the biggest lies that we are taught as children is that "sticks and stones break bones, but words do not hurt." On the con-trary—our words have the ability to inflict pain or pleasure. Other than our actions, words are the most valuable tool that we have when establishing and navigating intimate relationships. Words are extremely valuable, because they do not come with a return or exchange policy. Once you invest in the words you choose to give your partner, they will hold onto them for life.

Some people are more likely to respond to words and, for these individuals, what you say will literally make or break the relationship. In his book, Dr. Chapman describes how some partners need to hear certain words or phrases from each other in order to feel cared for. When these words are absent, they will not experience feeling loved. Partners who depend on affirming words need to hear more than just, "I love you." They need to experience their partner telling them *why* they love them, in order to completely feel cared for. In session, I direct couples to reflect on memories and share stories about how their partner made them feel valuable or cared for. Based on a partner's reaction while listening to their significant other sharing their feelings, I can gauge the importance of words. This was evident when I asked Jim to share in session what he experienced when he knew he wanted to propose to Mary. Jim shared that one evening he came home from work after a long day, and as soon as he laid eyes on Mary he felt a spiritual renewal from the sight of her beauty, eliminating any negative feelings he had harvested from work. He went on to share that Mary was the first person he ever met who could speak to his soul by simply looking him in the eyes. After Mary heard these words, she jumped across the couch into Jim's arms with tears flowing down her face. Jim was shocked by Mary's reaction. We then discussed the power his words obviously held when it came to ensuring that Mary feels cared for by him. Prior to therapy, Jim had underestimated the power of his words, and Mary had never shared how important it was for her to hear affirming sentiments from Jim.

Quality Time

Our time is the greatest gift we have, because time is life. When you choose to give your intimate partner your time, you are choosing to give them a piece of your life. Let's point out that Dr. Chapman specifically used the word "quality" and not quantity when listing time as one of his love languages. Many couples have routines that involve simply spending a bunch of time together, but that is more often *quantity* time and not *quality* time. Quality time is planned, intentional, and specifically designed to enhance intimacy. Quality time is a valuable tool that enables couples to sustain connection during adverse periods throughout their lives.

My wife and I are prime examples on how quality time can assist couples with remaining close throughout the pursuit of education, career changes, long distances, mental illness, and child-rearing. I met my wife online, and we established a long-distance relationship while we both pursued undergraduate degrees three hours apart. From the beginning of our courtship, we coined the term "every thirteen days," which meant we would never go more than thirteen days without spending at least two full, complete, uninterrupted days together. These usually fell on a week-end. Our quality time formula evolved with the relationship, and we strategically planned out our time together based on daily, weekly, and annual schedules. Every year during the last two weeks of December, we establish our relationship quality time plan for the upcoming year. Our plan includes a daily cutoff time when we will stop what we're doing and connect about our days. We have one weekly breakfast date, four days a month where we don't work and spend the day doing a planned activity (which we call "date days"), and an annual couples' getaway usually around the time of my wife's birthday. I feel like our quality time plan is the most exciting and fulfilling part of our marriage, because we choose to exchange valuable pieces of our life with each other routinely.

Gift Giving

We are taught that when giving gifts, it is the thought that counts—but this concept is never fully explained. The thoughts of both the giver and receiver hold equal value. When we give our intimate partner a gift, it should be something special meaning to them, in order to demonstrate our care for them. Doing this competently proves that we take an interest in our intimate partner's hobbies and desires. I find that partners who label gift giving as one of their primary love languages will enter therapy feeling not cared for based on the absence of gifts or gifts that do not meet their expectations. The quality of the gift is in the eye of the receiver, and not the giver. If your partner desires expensive gifts to feel cared for, then it's your job to find the means to provide them. In other words, people have the right to want what they want and like what they like.

Far too often, couples attempt to change their partner or hope their partner's gift-giving needs will change. This was the case for Jakobe and Ebony, who displayed different gift-giving expectations, which ultimately led to the end of their relationship. When Jakobe met Ebony, he was working at a job in a big city, making a lot of money. He was able to shower Ebony with expensive gifts and take her on several exotic vacations. Ebony was under the impression that she had met a man who shared her value for the finer things in life. After two years of dating, the couple got married—but this was also around the time things changed financially in their relationship. Jakobe lost his employment because it was a contracted position and the project concluded. He was unable to find the same caliber of employment, and had to settle for a position that produced a quarter of the previous salary he was making for the past three years. He informed Ebony that they had to scale back on vacations, and he was unable to sustain the expensive gift-giving habits that she had become accustomed to during the first two years of their relationship. Within three months of beginning life on their new budget, Ebony was developing disdain for Jakobe because he was unable to purchase expensive gifts. I recall Ebony sharing in session that she felt like Jakobe hadn't been fully forthcoming with her for the first two years of their relationship, and she was now forced to change her standards because he changed jobs. I found this couple's situation profound, because Ebony had shared at the beginning of the relationship that she needed and expected nice gifts from Jakobe in order to feel cared for. Jakobe stated that he thought he could alter Ebony's expectations once they fell in love and got married. He was wrong, and the couple later divorced due to Ebony not receiving what she needed to feel cared for.

To some reading this it may sound like Ebony put a lot of merit on expensive gifts—and she did but that is her choice. We cannot attempt to manage our partner's wants, needs, and desires. All we can do is select a mate who shares our same expectations and values, and educate each other on what these expectations look like at all times—including in moments of adversity.

Acts of Service

Out of all of Dr. Chapman's five love languages, performing acts of service is the most meaningful for couples who choose to inter-twine their lives together. One of the purposes of establishing an intimate relationship is that living with a partner makes your life a little easier. Some examples of the amenities provided by a relationship are when your partner prepares your food after a long day at work, performs chores around the house, or volunteers to wash your car without you asking. Acts of service demonstrate care because they give you an opportunity to address the needs of your partner and put them first. People who acknowledge acts of service as their primary love language value a partner who allows them to take the day off from doing chores, caring for children, or completing small errands—and being able to use that extra time to focus on themselves.

I find that these individuals also have a harder time receiving help, despite the fact that they desire it. Ryan and Leah are a prime example of a couple who experienced mild relationship conflict regarding the completion of service acts. Leah identified as a perfectionist, which prevented Ryan from engaging in service acts, because after he was done completing an act of service Leah would redo the task. Ryan shared several stories about how he would clean the house, wash their clothes, vacuum, and dust the furniture—and soon as Leah came home, she would redo every-thing he'd already done. Despite Ryan's attempts to serve his wife, upon entering therapy, Leah's major complaint was that she didn't feel like Ryan helped her around the house. While in couples therapy, Leah and Ryan both had a safe space with a trained professional to process their feelings. With tears flowing down her face Leah shared how, as a child, she could never clean the house or complete tasks that met her mother's approval. With hard work and dedication to the therapeutic process, Leah addressed her perfectionism and connected its origin to her mother, who had suffered from obsessive-compulsive disorder and depression. While going through this experience with Leah in couples therapy, Ryan was also able to gain a better understand about where his wife was coming from, which made it easier for him to process his built-up feelings of resentment, which stemmed from his feeling rejected when he attempted to complete acts of service.

Dr. Gary Chapman's *Five Love Languages* provides a basic template to ensuring couples feel cared for within their intimate relationships. When intimate partners do not feel cared for, they experience higher rates of disappointment, disconnection, disrespect, and feelings of being disregarded or ignored. These four problems wreak havoc on relationships if they are not quickly dissolved.

Problems That Develop When Intimate Partners Do Not Feel Cared For

The erosion of care between couples can easily start when one partner begins to feel disrespected by ongoing sarcastic comments that are meant to be taken as lighthearted jokes. The disrespected partner will attempt to express how they feel, but they are disregarded as being overly sensitive. As the hurt partner lingers in their disappointment because their feelings are not taken seriously, they can't help but to become disconnected from the relationship. In this context, there are four main factors which can lead to an inti-mate partner not feeling cared for in the relationship. These are:

- Disappointment
- Disconnection
- Disrespect
- Disregard

Disappointment

At some point during your intimate relationship, you should expect to be disappointed or let down by your partner—because nobody is perfect and life will happen. Due to unexpected circumstances, your intimate partner will fall short of meeting your expectations from time to time. This is normal. However, if you find your-self feeling disappointed by your intimate partner often, you will also start to feel like they do not care about you. When partners encounter disappointment, I find they usually activate four basic responses:

1. Giving them the benefit of the doubt
2. Expecting them to fail again

3. Keeping score while collecting ammunition
4. Turning toward others

Response 1
Benefit of the Doubt

Molly and Jim have been dating for six years and, while in premarital counseling, Molly stated that she experienced feeling disappointed by Jim only a few times over the entire course of their relationship. On these rare occasions, Molly's disappointment in Jim stemmed from the few times he defaulted on date night because of unexpected work projects that forced him to come home later than he intended. Jim shared that he could only count four or five times he felt disappointed by Molly, and they all took place when she rejected his attempts to initiate sex. Both Molly and Jim have felt disappointed by each other but still choose to respond by giving each other the benefit of the doubt.

Giving our partner the benefit of the doubt means making a decision to trust that, based on their track record, they did not intentionally mean to hurt us. In order to give your partner this response you have to first believe they care about you and the relationship. Secondly, your partner must earn this type of response by establishing habits of following through, consistently demonstrating acts of care, and taking responsibility by seeking reconciliation when they do make you feel disappointed. Molly stated that she felt like the few times Jim canceled on date night, he never intended to put his work before her. She also went on to share that, on those occasions where he canceled, he always rescheduled their date night. Jim mentioned in session that he easily got over his disappointment during the times Molly rejected his request for sex because she always made good on her rain checks. Molly and Jim respond to relationship disappointment by giving each other the benefit of the doubt. Giving your partner the benefit of doubt is possible when your disappointments or relationship letdowns can be seen as "just not right now" instead of "never." The partners who can give each other the benefit of the doubt believe in their intentions to always make each other feel cared for, and their actions consistently align with these intentions, which makes it easier for them both to move past disappointments.

Response 2
Expecting Failure

When your partner's track record is filled with broken promises, you will respond to disappointment with an expectation that your partner will let you down. This "expecting your partner to fail" response is used as a protection mechanism in order to prepare yourself emotionally for the impact of disappointment. The danger with this response is that, over time, your partner will stop put-ting forth an effort to please you because they will feel like you stopped caring. When Susan came into couples counseling without her partner present, she told me we should expect him to be late because he is late for everything involving her. John joined us in session a few minutes later and I read my informed consent documents that outline the conduct I expect my clients to follow in order to ensure they receive the highest quality of care. I shared with John and Susan that I expected them both to arrive on time for sessions, and if they were unable to commit to this expectation than I would not be a good fit as their couples therapist. The next session, John arrived on time and Susan was shocked. The couple engaged in a dialogue that went something like this:

Susan: Why are you on time for therapy and always late to every-thing else?

John: I care enough to be on time for therapy because I do not want to find another therapist.

Susan: What would it take for you to start caring more about our relationship and being on time for me? The fear of having to find another wife?

John: I stopped caring about you when you stopped caring about me.

Susan: Explain.

John: You used to ask me questions about why or what happened when I arrived late. I then got to share with you all the craziness that happened at work, which made me feel like you cared about what I was going through. Now you don't say anything, so I figured you stopped caring.

Susan: I never stopped caring, I just got tired of nagging and complaining about you being late all the time.

John: I didn't take your inquiries as nagging. I looked forward to your questions, because you were the only one who gave a damn about what happened to me.

Susan: I still do care. It just hurts to be waiting on your partner because they don't care enough about you to be on time.

John: I didn't know me being late caused you to feel like I stopped caring. I thought you understood I was late because of work stuff. You never displayed any anger and always listened to me explain what happened, which led me to believe there was not a problem.

Moving forward I will put forth an effort to be on time, but you have to let me know how you really feel.

Susan: That means a lot to me to hear you say that, because this whole time I thought you stopped caring about me and that's why you were late.

John: If I stopped caring about you, I wouldn't have made this commitment to come to counseling to repair our marriage. I love you.

John thought Susan stopped caring when she started to expect him to fail. When we stop holding our partners accountable, we do stop caring. If we stop striving for a better outcome, it means we care less than we once did.

Response 3
Keeping Score and Collecting Ammunition

When we attempt to ignore relationship disappointment and allow our negative feelings to build, while keeping a tally of all of the times our partners disappoint us, we are collecting ammunition that will be used during the next argument. Emotional ammunition builds up each time we suppress our true feelings of disappointment. This happens when we tell our partner something was no big deal when, in fact, it was. Perhaps they didn't ask if we had dinner prior to coming home with takeout for just themselves. We really are upset deep down inside, and hungry, but we tell our partner it's not a problem. Partners who fear being seen as empathetic are more likely to push aside their own feelings of disappointment and shrug off their partner's lack of care. The problem with this response is that disappointment, like all feelings, is equivalent to energy in that it cannot be created or destroyed, but only transferred from one form to another. Feelings of disappoint-ment transform into either understanding or resentment. Couples who attempt to ignore or put aside their feelings of disappointment without processing them with their partner are choosing to be resentful in the future. Resentment makes it easier to fire off insults when you get upset, because you have built up a stockpile of emotional ammunition. When we insult our partners, for any reason, they will feel like we do not care about them. When disappointment is not properly expressed, it morphs into anger, which causes more harm to the relationship. Instead, couples need to choose understanding—this includes educating your partner on your needs, wants, and expectations so they know how to respond next time to limit disappointment from occurring.

Response 4
Turning Toward Others

It's natural to have a preference for attempting to fix our own problems but, if we're not careful, our solutions can create issues bigger than the original problem. This is the case when intimate partners seek relief from disappointment by turning to people out-side of their relationship who are not trained professionals. These people tend to be family members, coworkers, or friends. Although their intentions may be good, they tend to cause more problems than good.

Brian's girlfriend called him selfish and he became disappointed by her remarks, because he always pays when they go on dates. Brian sought the opinion of a female coworker to help him cope with his feelings of disappointment, and to gain an ally who disagrees with his girlfriend. His coworker shared with him that she thinks he is a good man and that his girlfriend is unappreciative. Although Brian was pleased to hear someone else validate him, he was not satisfied seeking affirmation from only one source, so he called his mother. Brian's mother provided the ultimate cure to his disappointment, telling him that his girlfriend is wrong because, as his mother, she knows she did not raise a selfish son. Brian then felt empowered with affirmations from two females whose opinions he values, and he confronted his girlfriend to tell her she was wrong, and he is not selfish. After learning that their personal conversation was shared with others, Brian's girlfriend was infuriated and embarrassed. She asked Brian how he expected her to feel now that his coworker and mother thought he was dating an "ungrateful women"? Brian was stunned by her remarks and responded that all he was trying to do was convince her that he is not selfish. Brain's girlfriend responded by saying, "No, you wanted to convince yourself you are not selfish, this was not about me, it was about you!" In that moment, Brian understood why his girlfriend called him selfish, but it was too late. His girlfriend felt betrayed and chose to end the relationship.

Brian chose to turn to others outside of his relationship to assist him with not feeling disappointed by his girlfriend's comment. In the process, Brain demonstrated that he cared more about his personal feelings and pursued actions with only himself in mind. Brian's inability to secure privacy, coupled with not taking into consideration how his actions might affect his intimate partner, both lead to the end the relationship.

Why Therapy Helps

Intimate partners who have experienced a countless number of disappointing moments within their relationship turn to couples counseling as their last hope. Sometimes, these partners hope that counseling will fix their relationship by changing their significant other. Couples counseling will not change the person you are with, but does change the relationship you have with the person. Therapists focus on rewriting the rules of the relationship system in order to produce sustainable outcomes. The therapist will first start by assessing the relationship to find trends and themes that can be altered.

A common theme couples bring into therapy involves one partner who is always late. Kim and Roger had been married for fifteen years and, over the course of their relationship, Kim became notorious for being late. Roger stated during therapy that he attempted to give Kim earlier start times to help her with planning, but she still would arrive late. At one point, Roger tried meeting Kim at the house so that they could drive together, but his plan only resulted in them both being late due to Kim taking a longer time to leave. After assessing the couple's issue with time management, it was identified that Kim's tardiness came from a place of power and control. Roger was the family planner who scheduled all the dates, appointments, and reservations. Roger singlehandedly stepped into the scheduler role at the beginning of the relationship because he did not believe Kim was responsible enough to assist with managing the family calendar. During one of our sessions, Kim expressed that, over time, she began to feel like one of their children instead of Roger's equal. She admitted that being late or having the power to dictate when they arrived somewhere gave her a sense of control, even if it was at the expense of punctuality. As a therapeutic intervention, I assigned the couple homework that entailed Kim having more responsibility around planning start times, appointments, and organizing family outings. Within a few weeks the couple reported a drastic change where Kim and the entire family were more punctual to all their scheduled events.

Therapy assists couples with managing disappointments by helping intimate partners find the root causations for their undesirable symptoms. Once the underlying issues are exposed, the therapist will implement interventions that alter how the members of the system interact. This approach can produce a change in which the entire system chooses to reauthor their rules of engagement. Couples therapy changes the entire system, which in turn produces new outcomes. This approach can be applied to several different issues, problems, and concerns that couples bring into therapy. Systemic couples therapists view the sum of the relationship system as greater than one single person, which makes this approach less about fixing a broken partner and more about fixing a broken system.

Four Steps of Managing Disappointment

1. **Be Direct** *Immediately inform your partner (only them; not others) you are feeling disappointed, so they are aware of your cur-rent emotional state and are no longer operating on assumptions or attempting to read your mind.*

2. **Be Clear** *Specifically explain the actions, words, or thoughts that lead to your feelings of disappointment with your partner, and the supplemental emotions you are experiencing.*

3. **Check-Ins** *Request feedback from your partner as a check-in with their emotional status after they learn why their actions caused you to feel disappointed.*

4. **Hold Each Other Accountable** *Use the current dis-appointment as a catalyst to establish or add to the relationship boundaries, rules, and expectations for you and your partner to follow in order to prevent future disappointments from occurring*

Disconnection

Most people have heard at some point in their life the phrase "relationships take work," but very few are given a clear definition for what that work looks like. The work is the effort both partners put forth to stay connected and prevent coming apart. Just like an astronaut who enters space works against the lack of gravity to stay tethered to something in order to prevent flying off into space, couples have to work constantly against the four forces of time management, external factors, change in direction, and negative feelings—or they will find themselves miles apart despite living in the same home. Disconnection is the most important factor that leads couples to feeling uncared for by their intimate partner. I have heard couples say they "just grew apart," or that the spark has gone out. These phrases represent the absence of the work required to sustain connection. In his book *The Relationship Cure*, Dr. John Gottman writes that arguments do not create disconnection, but instead disconnection produces more intensified conflict. It becomes easier to say mean things to your partner when the relationship connection is impeded. You will find yourself listening less and yelling or lecturing more when you experience a breach in connection. Disconnection is the cancer that alters the relationship cells and turns laughter into tears, smiles into frowns, and misunderstandings into declarations of war. Couples have to be made aware of the four major sources of disconnection and then equip their relationship with the processes and procedures of screening, identifying, targeting, and removing the sources of disconnection.

The four primary forces of disconnection are: time management, external factors, change in direction, and negative feelings.

Time Management (The Four Quadrants)

Despite time being the only absolute in life, we still seem to miscalculate its use. Although we can plan out events on the minute or hour, we still seem never to have enough time to get all the things we desire completed. Based on Stephen Covey's book *The Seven*

Habits of Highly Effective People, there are four quadrants of time management which are defined by either the presence or absence of urgency and importance. The ways we interact with our inti-mate partner in each of these four quadrants of time management influence relationship connection and disconnection.

Quadrant 1: High Urgency and High Importance

The most hyperfunctioning quadrant is the high-urgency and high-importance aspect of time management, which is usually designated for tasks that require our immediate attention and time (such as emergencies). An example of demonstrating care for your intimate partner in this quadrant of high urgency and high importance would be rushing to their side to provide protection, comfort, or support if you find out that your partner has suffered some form of illness, hurt, harm, or danger. Despite the physical barriers present, connected couples do whatever it takes in order to be with their partner in their time of need. If you drag your feet or do not attempt to be with your partner in a timely fashion, they will instinctively question your level of care which is indicative to the relationship's degree of connection.

This was the case for Jake and Lisa. Jake had been experiencing a reduction in marital satisfaction for several years and, for a while, he was able to conceal his unhappiness by going through the motions of providing Lisa with meaningless gifts and empty words of affection. Jake's true feelings for Lisa were highlighted when she passed out at work and was rushed to the hospital. Jake was out of town on routine business when he got the news about Lisa and, despite the severity of his wife's health condition, Jake still chose to return home four days later as originally planned. When Jake arrived home, Lisa was still in the hospital and was diagnosed with a heart condition. Jake's lack of urgency to be by Lisa's side prompted her to feel uncared for and marked the beginning of the couple's marriage unraveling. Jake's inability to respond to Lisa with urgency during an important time communicated that he was completely checked out of the relationship and had little care for his wife. The way Jake chose to use his time in a highly urgent and important situation pertaining to his wife's health illustrated disconnection, which his wife interpreted as not feeling cared for.

Quadrant 2: Low Urgency and High Importance

The low-urgency and high-importance quadrant of time management is the most valuable place couples spend their time together. Here, intimate partners plan ways to stay connected and work to resolve issues, which are two major investments that move their relationship forward. Since this quadrant is low in urgency, it is easily overlooked, because most couples are reactive and not pro-active. Couples that are preemptive find it important to monitor their relationship connection status and develop procedures to reduce disconnection from happening. This can be couples who establish daily routines to talk about their relationship, engage in weekly date nights, take vacations, and set goals for their lives together.

When reflecting on my own marriage, I can identify moments when my wife and I had to fight against the forces of disconnection that stem from our pursuits of educational and professional achievements, geographical distances, childrearing, and moments when negative feelings or conflict arose. We were able to sustain connection during these events and phases of life together because of the time we invested in the low urgency and high importance quadrant. During our first few years of marriage, we established routines that consisted of reading and processing marital self-help books, videos, and worksheets. We were both extremely tired after work and caring for a toddler but, nevertheless, we fought through the fatigue and completed relationship developmental tasks, because we felt that this was important for our marriage. I have come to find that most of the couples I treat in therapy have never voluntarily completed relationship developmental tasks and are only prompted to do so when I assign them as homework. By the time these couples choose to enter therapy, they have developed layers of hurt, pain, and frustration which make it even harder to invest in the necessary time needed to repair the relationship. These damaged couples are working on their relationship during times of crisis and are attempting to make changes to their relationship in the high urgency and high importance quadrant. The problem these couples encounter is that, by the time they attempt the repair work needed to restore connection, the damage in some cases is far too great to treat with educational material. Couples who achieve the best outcomes in restoring and sustaining connection tend to work on their relationship during the low urgency and high importance time quadrant.

High Urgency and Low Importance

The high-urgency and low-importance quadrant of time management is the most deceptive place couples spend time together, because they are teaching each other that care is only valid during emergencies. Responses that are required to meet needs that are urgent but low in importance can feel like the distribution of care, but this process often leads to the development of codependency. Codependent couples consist of partners who take on the roles of problem producer and problem solver. The problem-producing partners often tend to find themselves in conflict, and develop a reliance on problem-solving partners to fix their issues. Initially, this routine appears to be sufficient, because the problem-producing partner gets relief and the problem-solving partner gains gratification from feeling needed. Over time, however, the codependent couple develops an emotional alliance that is sustained only by the need for problems to be solved. The problem-solving partner begins to feel lonely and starts to view the problem-producing partner as someone who is weak, needy, and unattractive.

This was the case for Jeremy and Rose, who came in to therapy after nine years of marriage. When the couple first met, Rose was an unemployed single mother who was recently divorced after spending four years married to an abusive, alcoholic husband. Jeremy had just hit his professional prime and was seeking companionship, but lacked the self-esteem and confidence needed to attract an independent mate. When the two began dating, Jeremy found pleasure in supporting Rose and her son, because it made him feel like a man to provide for others. Jeremy's connection to Rose deepened as she expressed her appreciation for his ability to fix her problems. He paid her bills and fulfilled coparenting responsibilities for her son who desperately needed the stability of a two-parent household. Jeremy asked Rose to marry him after just three months of dating, and at the time he felt good knowing he found someone who relied on him for the majority of their needs. As the couple's relationship evolved, Jeremy spent most of his time with Rose, assisting her in solving urgent but non important problems. Jeremy would come to the rescue every time—for example, if he was helping Rose look for a lost item she misplaced but he could not find it, he would purchase another one. In the event Rose engaged in conflict with others, Jeremy would jump in to "fix-it mode" and get involved as a mediator to help Rose manage the relationship conflict. Rose found a job, but was unable to sustain it because, when she got tired of reporting to work or upset at her manager, Jeremy never encouraged her not to give up and quit. In fact, he suggested each time that she just quit her job because his business made more than enough money to support the entire family.

The couple's relationship took a drastic turn after Jeremy was diagnosed with a life-threating illness and he was no longer capable of responding to Rose's problems with the same level of urgency. As a result, Rose began to criticize Jeremy when she felt like he was no longer immediately rushing to her aid. Rose's expectations for Jeremy to rescue her did not lessen, despite him enduring chemotherapy treatments needed to save his life while he continued to work in order to support the entire family financially. Jeremy began to question his value as a man, because he did not have any leftover energy to solve Rose's problems. The couple built the marriage on the foundation of the time they spent together in the high-urgency and low-importance quadrant, and this was no longer an ideal place for them after Jeremy's health issues became urgent and important. The couple's level of disconnection intensified and influenced Jeremy to seek out sex workers as a means of finding the validation he once received from Rose. After Rose contracted a sexually transmitted disease because of Jeremy's infidelity, she chose to dissolve the marriage. This couple is a prime example of how spending time exclusively in the high-urgency and low-importance quadrant can lead to disconnection and not feeling cared for.

Low Urgency and Low Importance

The low-urgency and low-importance quadrant of time management is designated for tasks that do not warrant any urgency or importance. This could include spending the whole day watching a new television series with your partner. Watching television is not an urgent or important task, but can produce a shared euphoric experience which can support connection. The low-urgency and low-importance quadrant of time within the relationship can be seen like dessert. It is good in moderate amounts, but if overly relied upon it can create relationship cavities and malnourishment.

Linda and Sam met at a club and hooked up for a drunken one-night stand that turned into a fling. Sam enjoyed the time he got to spend with Linda, because of the freedom he had to cut his brain off and just have fun. The couple never talked about their feelings, life plans, interests, hobbies, or past experiences, but instead they focused on making their time together as fun as possible. They went to theme parks, movies, and partook of a lot of tele-vision and sex. After about the three-month period, Linda asked Sam if they could be exclusive and begin the process of taking the relationship to the next level. Sam responded with laughter and asked Linda why she would make such a silly request, because they barely knew each other. Linda stated that they had been spending the past three months together and she thought a connection was forming. Sam asked Linda how she could feel connected to him when she really knew nothing about him? He then began to rattle off basic questions pertaining to his family, occupation, hobbies, interests, and personal values, which Linda could not even begin to answer. Linda felt embarrassed and asked Sam to leave her apartment at once. Sam politely obliged by grabbing his jacket and, on his way out, he told Linda it had been fun, and he wished her the best.

I met Linda for individual therapy while interning as a therapist graduate student in the school's community outpatient mental health clinic. Linda sought out therapy to learn how she had misread the relationship cues which prompted her to feel a connection that was nonexistent for Sam. We identified in therapy that Linda was raised by divorced parents, and she recalled how her father would spend a lot of time with her doing low-urgency and low-importance tasks such as going to the movies and other fun activities. Linda could not recall any times she and her father engaged in deep or thought-provoking conversations. When reflecting on Linda's past relationships, she stated that they usually ended once the fun and excitement subsided. This is a common theme for couples who attempt to build intimate relationships based on the time they spend in the low-urgency and low-importance quadrant. The reason these relationships wear off so quickly is because they mirror a sugar rush. When we eat large amounts of sugar, we experience a spike in energy followed by a crash which is prompted by a flood of insulin. The sugar analogy in Linda's relationships was represented by an influx of fun, followed by the reality that she never took the time to get to know the person she was with. From therapy, Linda developed a new process for dating which involved spending more time in the low-urgency and high-importance quadrant. In the low-urgency and high-importance quad-rant Linda was able to spend time getting to know her partners and deciphering factors that could be used to determine if a true connection was forming.

External Factors

External factors are another source of disconnection that intimate partners have to work to manage in order to sustain a close relation-ship that exhibits care. The most common examples of external relationship factors are kids and extended family members. Kids immediately decrease the amount of alone time couples will have. Couples who are trying to get pregnant should start planning ways to stay connected after the kids are born. It takes time to readjust your life upon the arrival of a new addition, and planning time to be alone together is a necessary antidote for the distance that kids produce between intimate partners. Couples who establish prearranged support systems—such as a trusted network of family and friends, childcare, and babysitters—do a better job at sustaining a connection, because they can schedule alone time together.

I know from firsthand experience that if it was not for our family, babysitter, and childcare center, my wife and I would never have alone time without our kids to work out at the gym, have a date night, or play hooky from work and spend the whole day together. Trusted family members can play a role in supporting relationship connection, but they can also operate as a disconnector when not properly managed. If your partner is extremely close to their parents or siblings and tends to confide in them before you, you may feel like you are the last to hear about some things despite your important role in your partner's life. You may also feel like your partner is more responsive to their family and will heed their advice over yours.

These two experiences, if gone unchecked, will create disconnection over time because of built-up resentment. This was the case for Carter and Amber, who sought out premarital counseling. Amber was concerned because she felt like Carter turned to his mother and father when it came time to make decisions about their relationship. She stated that Carter sought out their opinions more than hers as they planned their wedding. After hearing Amber express her feelings, Carter became defensive and stated that Amber was just acting like a drama queen and was jealous of the relationship he had with his parents. We spent a lot of time in therapy normalizing both partners' experiences based on their different families of origin. Amber did not grow up in a close-knit family and was overwhelmed by the level of involvement Carter's parents had in his life. Carter was unaware that his parents were using their influential power in a self-serving manner to get him to make decisions that favored them— for example, suggesting that he ask Amber if his side of the family could host twenty-five additional guests despite the couple agreeing they would invite an equal number of people. Carter's parents even attempted to impose their input on the wedding venue and location, until Amber stood her ground on getting married at her childhood church located in the small rural town in which she was raised. Therapy assisted Carter and Amber by equipping them with the tools, information, and procedures required to sustain healthy boundaries with family. As a result, the couple enhanced their relationship connection and increased their feelings of care.

Change in Direction

Sometimes in life we will have our plans altered, but if we want to reach our full potential and arrive at a place we define as successful then we must learn how to change directions. The same can be applied to couples who wish to stay connected, despite a reroute or unexpected change of direction. Abrupt life changes that modify the direction in which a couple is headed include events like unexcepted pregnancy, the relocation of a job, major physical or mental health illnesses, changes in finances, or a new development in the pursuit of individual life goals and dreams. These unplanned changes can create disconnection, because relationships take on an identity that has an impact on the current place in life in which both partners see themselves. Some partners do not want to make those changes together, resulting in the creation of space. When too much space is produced, the relationship can come apart. It is not uncommon to see couples in therapy who are at a cross-roads when it comes to deciding if they should go through with an unplanned pregnancy or get an abortion. This is an example of a "make it or break it" scenario that will either produce a stronger connection or the start of disconnection. In session, couples therapists will work with the couple to process each partner's beliefs, needs, wants, and expectations so that they can make the best decisions for their relationship. It should be made known that the decision to continue with or terminate a pregnancy is ultimately a woman's decision, since it is her body.

Once a couple consents to have sex, they are also consenting to the consequences of that action, which may include pregnancy. Claudia and Ricardo initiated therapy once they became pregnant unexpectedly, after dating for just ten months. The couple lived four hours apart and only spent time together once every two weeks due to the demands of their hectic work schedules. Claudia was a seasoned banker in her mid-thirties who was excited about the pregnancy because she felt like her window to be a mother was closing. Although Claudia did not intend on becoming pregnant and she fell in the category of the small per-cent of women who conceive while using an intrauterine device (IUD), she was able to embrace the idea of parenthood with positive emotions. Claudia also felt like she and Ricardo shared a meaningful connection, which allowed her to be at peace with having their baby. Ricardo, on the other hand, approached the pregnancy like a death sentence and demanded that Claudia abort the pregnancy at once.

Ricardo stated that he refused to be like his parents, who chose to accelerate their relationship because they got pregnant with him unexpectedly. He shared how his childhood was plagued by living with two people who had nothing in common outside of raising him. Claudia was confused when hearing this, because she felt like she and Ricardo's relationship was different, since it was founded on common interests, life goals, and beliefs. Later, during our therapeutic journey, we learned that Ricardo feared a change in life direction that might include relocating, having to change jobs, and having less time to get to know Claudia prior to fusing their lives together. The climax for both partners during therapy, which assisted them in making their final decision, came when Claudia revealed that she had had an abortion in the past, and she refused to endure that experience again. Claudia then proceeded to share that the only reservation she was having about the cur-rent pregnancy was the fear of being rejected by Ricardo. Ricardo shared that, despite how their relationship transpired, he would never abandon Claudia or their child. Therapy assisted Claudia by giving her permission to no longer feel like she had to be responsible for Ricardo's feelings. She was attempting to control Ricardo's reaction to the pregnancy by operating from a place of openness when she had already made up her mind to keep the baby.

When life alters a couple's journey, the choice to adapt and change direction is still an independent decision. We cannot control our partner's actions or responses—just our own.

Negative Feelings

It should go without saying that if two people stay together long enough, there will be moments during the relationship where negative feelings will move in like clouds and block the sunshine of positivity. However, similar to the transitions that occur in nature, couples have to remember that the clouds of negative feelings will eventually move out and the sunrays of laughter and positivity will return.

When asking a client what her secret was for sustaining a forty-year marriage, she responded by saying she and her husband never both fell out of love at the same time during the course of the marriage. I believe she was alluding to the fact that, if you're married long enough, there will be periods where you are not going to be as fond of your partner—but in order to sustain the relationship, you cannot submit to allowing extended periods of time to pass without reconciliation.

Why Therapy Helps

When treating couples who report experiencing negative feelings toward each other, one of the ways therapy helps is by shortening the time between reconciliation. This includes reducing the couple's recovery time when negative feelings arise because of minor events such as when one partner makes a snappy remark or fails to put their clothes in the hamper. In more extreme situations, such as betrayal or infidelity where the hurt runs deeper, one or both partners may need extended time for healing to take place. Even during moments when partners need longer periods to heal, the couples who stay together learn how to give and receive repair attempts. Dr. John Gottman defines a repair attempt as "any statement or action, verbal, physical, or otherwise, meant to diffuse negativity and keep a conflict from escalating out of control." When couples fail to embrace repair attempts, they allow the rain of negative feelings to flood the relationship. The relationship environment can then get moldy because of distance, disgust, dis-pleasure, and disinterest. Negative feelings arise in each partner at some point during the relationship, and the couples who submit to their negative feelings for extended periods of time become dis-connected. Therapy helps couples learn how to deploy and receive repair attempts so they can dissolve negative feelings before dis-connection sets in.

The Four Signs of Relationship Disconnection

1. **Distance** The failure to sustain some form of inti-mate connection due to unavoidable separation caused by work schedules, military deployment, or other life moments which require the two partners to be physically

apart for extended, moderate, or even short amounts of time.

2. ***Disgust*** Negative thoughts, feelings, and emotions that occur when engaging with your intimate partner, but which go away once you are separated from each other.

3. ***Displeasure*** The inability to feel joy, happiness, or any positive emotions when speaking to or spending time with your intimate partner.

4. ***Disinterest*** A lack of stimulation that can result in spending more time with others who you feel provide a higher level of satisfaction.

Disrespect

If you or your partner communicate messages that are coded as devaluing, insulting, or belittling, then feelings of disrespect will follow. When people feel disrespected by their intimate partner, they also do not feel cared for. Disrespect is interpreted differently based on cultural, societal, and personal beliefs, which makes it sometimes challenging to identify. This is especially true for couples who fail to verbally express when and why they feel disrespected by each other. Uninformed partners are unable to correct disrespectful behaviors, and they continue the same disrespectful actions that drive their mate further away from them.

Not all disrespectful actions are intentional and, in my work as a couples therapist, I find that most couples experience higher levels of disrespect during the formative years of the relationship as they work to figure each other out. This was apparent in my own marriage as well, and produced a constant feeling of walking on eggshells during the first few years. I recall feeling like everything I did was wrong and caused my wife to feel disrespected or upset. One time we met two other couples at a restaurant and, as we were all leaving, the other husbands held the door for their wives.

Instead, I walked ahead toward the valet station. My plan was to get the car pulled around faster before it started raining, because my wife just got her hair styled that morning and I knew that if it got wet, she would be very disappointed. The whole car ride home my wife was giving me the silent treatment and, when I asked what was wrong, she told me how she had felt disrespected because I was the only husband who didn't hold the door. I explained my intentions to get the car before it started raining because I didn't want her hair to get wet. She completely understood and thanked me for thinking about her in that way. This example represents how we can misinterpret our partner's actions as disrespectful. I have since learned that a lot of couples experience feeling disrespected when they do not feel safe, heard, understood, or cared for by their intimate partner. Your intimate partner will feel the most disrespected when you put them in a position of danger, embarrass them, make yourself unavailable, take them for granted, or challenge their autonomy.

Why Therapy Helps

Couples who report feeling disrespected by their partner tend to seek therapy to find relief from behaviors that make them feel less than, insulted, or belittled. During the assessment phase of counseling, the therapist is made aware of these behaviors and ensures that both partners are safe enough to share how they feel. It is common for partners to defend their disrespectful behaviors as a joke, but it is no laughing matter when someone feels hurt by our words or actions. In the event one partner attempts to sidestep the severity of their distrustful behaviors, the therapist will take a supportive stance and highlight the painful emotions their significant other feels. Once the disrespected partner acknowledges how their comments and actions have damaged the intimate relationship, the couple is then ready to cross over into the expletory phase. During the expletory phase, the therapist assists the disrespectful partner with identifying the origins of their hurtful behaviors.

Therapists start by processing the client's upbringing, and often find that one or both parents introduced the disrespectful behaviors to the client during their formative years. This was the case for Brian, who constantly made remarks toward his wife Martha, who found his comments over time to be disrespectful and obnoxious. Initially, when the couple entered therapy, Brian attempted to dismiss Martha's reactions to his remarks as her not being able to take a joke. Brian's thought process changed after therapy helped him link his disrespectful behaviors to his father. Brian described his dad as someone who constantly picks on and insults others for sport. He shared how, during family and social engagements, no one enjoyed being around his dad because he was constantly pointing out everyone's shortcomings. Brain further expressed how he too disliked the comments his dad made toward him about his weight, the clothes he wore, and the job he worked. Brian continued by expressing that his dad was the only one who thought the remarks to be funny, and would always end his statements by saying he was just joking. When Brian was done speaking about his dad, the therapy room was filled with silence as he and Martha sat in a reflective daze. After a few moments had passed, Martha turned to Brain and said, "When you make hurtful comments, it feels like you are acting like your father and I do not want to be around you." Brian stopped his disrespectful behaviors toward Martha after he was able to empathize with how his actions made his wife feel. Therapy helped the couple become closer, because Martha no longer feared feeling disrespected by Brian's sarcastic and hurtful comments.

The Four Types of Disrespect

1. *Endangerment* **Placing your intimate partner in a position that threatens their physical, mental, or emotional health and well-being.**

   Speaking to your partner in a loud or aggressive tone; embarrassing your partner in public by using sarcasm or disclosing private information; failing to honor the monogamy commitment or relationship boundaries and agreements.

2. *Detaching* **Deliberately choosing to ignore, neglect, or abandon your intimate partner when they seek your time and attention.**

   Failing to make your partner a priority or putting others outside of the relationship first; shutting down or stonewalling during emotionally arousing conversations; choosing to improperly take space by leaving without letting your partner know where you'll be and what time you plan on returning.

3. *Devaluing* **Exhibiting actions or words toward your intimate partner that make them feel ashamed, insecure, humiliated, or degraded.**

   Interrupting or cutting your partner off when they are speaking; neglecting to clean up after yourself and refusing to do household chores; failing to contribute to the shared responsibilities of child-rearing.

4. *Domineering* **Attempting to control or dictate your intimate partner's thoughts, feelings, words, or actions.**

   Making important decisions without consulting your partner; telling your partner how they should feel or think; ignoring your partner's dreams and goals; deliberately sabotaging your partner's attempts at being seen as an individual first and an intimate partner second.

Disregard

Humans are designed to be social beings and, as a result, we enjoy the exchange of attention that accompanies human interaction. However, when involved in an intimate relationship, the time and attention we often desire most of all is that of our intimate partner. When we do not receive our partner's care, we begin to feel disregarded and ignored. These feelings can easily snowball into questions about whether our partner values us or if they desire to stay in the relationship. Couples seek therapy to get answers to questions that stem from their partner's general interest in them and the relationship. Partners tend to develop these questions when they notice changes in behaviors that make them feel unseen, unheard, mistreated, and undervalued. When these feelings arise in the relationship, it is to be expected that intimate partners will not feel properly cared for by each other.

Why Therapy Helps

Intimate partners who feel disregarded come to therapy because they are contemplating whether the relationship is worth sustaining. These partners share that the only time they engage with each other is when they are fighting or arguing. I find that these couples have been in a bad place for a long time and simply do not know how to get out of the self-inflicted hell they created. Underneath all the pain, they are still able to find some flicker of hope that influenced them both to seek out therapy before the relationship became unrepairable. Therapy initially helps these couples by assisting them with establishing codes of conduct that stop the emotional bleeding long enough for their wounds to be treated.

This process is called crisis management, and entails helping the couple identify relationship strengths they can use to restore value and hope. Couples are reminded of their partner's loyalty to monogamy, desire to provide, or ability to successfully coparent— these factors encourage them to fight for the relationship. The therapist will then begin the process of Emotionally Focused Therapy (EFT) techniques and interventions. EFT is a research-based therapeutic approached designed by Dr. Sue Johnson who is also the author of the bestseller *Hold Me Tight*. EFT is the top-rated therapeutic modality, designed to turn intimate partners back toward each other by identifying and treating attachment wounds. Attachment wounds are occurrences in the relationship that drove the couple apart and made it unsafe to sustain connection. EFT helps the couple restore security, connection, and closeness so that partners no longer feels disregarded and ignored.

The Four Actions that Produce Feeling Disregarded

1. *Undetected* **Failing to acknowledge your partner's physical and emotional presences in your life.**
    Reentering the home after any length of time away and forgetting or refusing to greet your partner with a physical or verbal acknowledgment; making social, recreational, or occupational plans without soliciting your partner's opinion and including their feedback in the decision-making process.

2. *Ignoring* **Forgetting or not hearing what your partner verbally shared or requested because of the absence of active listening.**
    Preparing your response or thinking about something else while your partner is speaking; being unable to recite what you just heard your partner say; delivering

large volumes of information, instead of short packets; speaking as if pouring an entire pitcher, instead of one shot glass.

3. *Mistreating* **Responding to your partner in any manner perceived to be abusive, neglectful, or manipulative.**

   Continuing a behavior after your partner tells you to stop or informs you that the action causes them pain; choosing not to practice the platinum rule—"treat people the way they want to be treated."

4. *Undervaluing* **Neglecting to communicate appreciation for your intimate partner's contributions and overall presence in your life.**

   Operating from a position of entitlement; expecting your partner to meet your needs and wants without showing them any form of gratitude; allowing time or comfort to erode good habits like saying *please* and *thank you.*

Barriers That Block Intimate Partners from Feeling Cared For

After couples have diagnosed and treated relationship problems pertaining to feeling cared for, they still may encounter internal barriers that prevent them from displaying care for each other. These barriers are internal because they originate from feelings that come from within, which are designed to protect us in the midst of conflict. When we feel like our partner has gone a while without fulfilling our needs and wants, we can become selfish. Selfishness is designed to assist us with preserving our ego so we will have self-value left over to give at a later time. If we go too long feeling like our partner does not care for us, then our selfishness can turn into resentment. We may start to resent being alone and seek out companionship from sources that do not provide long-lasting fulfillment. This might include engaging in affairs, one-night stands, or supporting relationships that we know have limited potential. Coming to our senses and embracing the impact of reality can plunge us into regret. Regret is the realization that our past choices were not designed to set us up for future successes. In order to effectively treat our regret, we have to face the fears of our past, present, and future. We will not be able to truly care for another person until we knock down the following barriers:

- Selfishness
- Resentment
- Regret
- Fear

Selfishness

The act of being selfish derives from our protection system for survival, which instinctively guides us toward what we need and want to sustain life. However, selfishness can be like a computer firewall, blocking our pathways to establishing caring and intimate relationships. Selfishness limits the capacity for compromise, compassion, companionship, and consideration for others. It takes time for couples to pull back their layers of selfishness, and can require patience from both partners when first forming a relationship.

Couples therapists assist intimate partners with the process of becoming less selfish by building trust, which is a major tool used to peel off the film of selfishness. I often meet couples who are in the first five years of courtship or marriage and, while in therapy, we reflect on phases of their lives prior to the relationship that required them to develop a higher degree of selfishness. (For example, earning degrees, career training, ending a toxic relationship, becoming sober from alcohol or drugs, single parenting, poverty or homeless-ness, and detaching from parents, disablers, or abusers.)

Mike and Mary were a couple I treated for premarital counseling who demonstrated a few of the classic factors that promote selfishness. One year prior to their engagement, Mike completed his doctorate degree and concluded a five-year journey that forced him to spend countless hours alone conducting research and writing papers about his findings. Before starting his educational odyssey, Mike ended a three-year marriage he defined as one-sided, because his ex-wife only took what he offered and never gave anything in return. Mike was now fresh out of graduate school and was ready to give marriage another try, but the residue from negative feelings brought on by his past marriage—and his "me against the world" mentality that he developed while in graduate school— covered him in a strong layer of selfishness that he was unaware even existed. Prior to meeting Mike, Mary was forced to become a single mother of a teenage son after her previous husband died from cancer, which also left her financially unstable because her husband did not have life insurance. Mary moved in with her parents to reduce expenses and enrolled in cosmetology school, despite the disapproval of her mother, who wanted her to become a schoolteacher. Mary became a successful hairstylist and beauty shop owner. She was able to build her dream home and detach from the toxic relationship she had with her mother who constantly spewed verbal criticisms regarding Mary's career and life choices.

Why Therapy Helps

The primary issues Mary and Mike brought into premarital counseling stemmed from making decisions pertaining to living arrangements, coparenting, and blended finances. The couple was having problems making these life-joining decisions because they refused to compromise and validate each other's feelings. At first, they attempted to solve their problems by reading books and information online, but continued to feel like the other was choosing to be selfish. When I first met with Mike, he stated the problem would go away if Mary would simply get rid of the prenuptial agreement requests, sell her house and move in with him, and allow him to parent the way he wanted to. After meeting with Mary independently, she echoed similar solutions involving Mike selling his house and moving in with her, signing the prenup argument, and following her parenting lead.

During therapy, the couple processed their histories of trust-ing previous partners who had left them both to fend for them-selves. Although Mary's husband did not plan on dying, he failed to protect his family by not taking out a life insurance policy. This led Mary to develop the belief that she had to protect herself and her son, since she produced more income than Mike. Mike trusted that his ex-wife would be his partner for life, but while married he only witnessed the act of giving without receiving anything in return. Mike's ex-wife took half of all his monetary assets during the divorce, which made it tough for him to consider marriage again with the potential of taking a financial hit if things did not work out. With a lot of work in therapy, Mike and Mary were able to learn how to trust each other and dismantle the barriers of selfishness that blocked compromise, compassion, companionship, and consideration for each other's feelings.

The Four Caring Behaviors Blocked by Selfishness

1. **Compromise** The ability for a couple to make a joint decision that renders a win-win outcome from which they both mutually benefit.
2. **Compassion** A demonstration of empathy that permits you to connect with the feelings your partner is currently experiencing.
3. **Companionship** A sense of togetherness joined by mutual interest, trust, liking, and concern for each other.
4. **Consideration** Deliberately submitting to your partner's requests and requirements with regard to how they want you to treat them.

Resentment

At some point in your relationship you will become upset with your partner and, if you fail to process your hurt, resentment will begin to grow. Resentment blocks care because it is similar to a record or CD that is scratched and prevents the song from playing beyond a single point. The music, which represents your emotions, will continue to repeat itself, preventing you and your intimate partner from enjoying the rest of the song, which is the relationship. Intimate partners who harness resentment are unable to get past feeling hurt or upset. Resentful partners are consumed by the pain they experienced and are trapped by their negative emotions. Whenever they think about the activating event that originally made them upset, they relive the trauma over, which creates even more anger. When working with couples in therapy, I find that resentment is the culprit for a lot of relationships that fail because it creates the rumination of negative thoughts, an inability to forgive, a victim mentality, and irresolvable tension.

Why Therapy Helps

The pain intimate partners experience when they are hurt emotion-ally will last as long as they choose for it to. If the hurt partner chooses to allow their pain to take over and control them, then it will. Once the pain begins the settle in, it will become a part of the relationship. This form of deep-rooted hurt will stain the relationship with resentment. Intimate partners who seek couples therapy to treat resentment have to first be willing to let go. Letting go is a process that can take time, and therapy is used to guide the couple toward a destination that extracts the pain from the stain of resentment. The stain will always be present, but it does not have to keep hurting. Couples therapy invites the partner who caused the pain into the world of the hurt partner, so they are able to truly understand the depth of agony they caused. The hurt partner will never be able to start the process of letting go until they are able to believe that their significant other sincerely feels the same level of hurt. Not until then will they be able to feel safe enough to trust again. In therapy, the partner who has caused the pain is taught how to experience the pain alongside their significant other. The pain-provoking partner will be stained by their actions, because they will forever serve as a reminder of what they lost. Hurt partners can learn how to let go and forgive, but they will never be able to learn how to forget. Remembering what happened is the scar that will forever be a part of the relationship. That scar will represent the loss of the past relationship that existed prior to the pain and resentment taking place. Therapy helps couples knock down the barriers of resentment by replacing it with empathy and understanding. Despite all the work in therapy, couples will still have to choose if they are willing to live with a stain that is recalled when either partner is reminded of the pain-provoking event. For some partners I treat, the stain becomes a part of the couple's narrative and represents their resolve and reliance to make the relationship work no matter what. For others, the weight of resentment is too much to bear. Therapy assists couples with determining if their relationship is strong enough to replace hurt feelings with empathy, which is the antidote for treating resentment.

The Four Elements of Resentment

1. **Rumination on Negative Thoughts** The inability to move past the resurgence of negative emotions and feelings, which develop when reflecting on a damaging event in which your intimate partner caused you hurt or pain.
2. **Failure to Forgive** A lingering disbelief in your partner's understanding of how they hurt you, which in turn limits you from being vulnerable. A feeling like your partner will repeat the same pain-provoking actions in the future.
3. **Victim Mentality** A constant state of fear that prevents you from being open to experiencing physical, mental, or emotional intimacy between you and your partner.
4. **Irresolvable Tension** A long-standing absence of security, understanding, and hope that prohibits relationship repair and leads to both partners choosing to go their separate ways with no chance of reconciliation in the future.

Regret

We have all made choices or said things we wish we could take back but, due to our inability to travel backward in time and erase past actions, we are forced to live with regrets. Regret occurs when you revisit historical moments in your live and develop feelings of shame and guilt based on things you did or said that cannot be changed. Shame and guilt shape how you see yourself, which ultimately impacts how your intimate partner sees you. If you believe your-selves to be an embarrassment or disgrace, then your actions can become a self-fulfilling prophecy and bring these beliefs to reality. Your regrets produce a thought cycle fueled by feelings of shame and guilt, which cause poor decisions to be made. If you regret hurting a past intimate partner but fail to learn how your actions impact others, you will repeat the same actions, confirming you are a per-son who hurts those they care about. This process is similar to a hangover the night after a lot of drinking, because you regret the dis-comfort but not the drinking that caused it. To prevent regret from blocking your ability to demonstrate care for your intimate partner, you must learn from your regrettable choices and break the cycle.

Why Therapy Helps

Regret is like the swelling that occurs after we accept the consequence of an ill-advised choice. Therapy helps by applying an ice pack filled with empathy and understand to the couple, to reduce the swelling and break the cycle of pain. Both partners are given the first aid of being heard and listened to. Therapy helps by soothing the emotional bruises with the introspection needed to prevent future relationship contusions. The pain-provoking partner uses their words to wrap a stint of accountability around the hurt partner. The hurt partner's insight and emotional expressions are the cures the pain-provoking partner needs in order to alter their behavior. The therapist works like the hospital, to provide a stable environment for healing, all while staying out of the couple's way so that they can have a safe space to heal. Therapy helps treat regret by enhancing the sensitivity of the couple's emotional receptors so insight and understanding can be better absorbed.

The Four Steps Toward Dissolving Relationship Regret

1. **Recognition** Acknowledging to your intimate partner that you are aware of the words or actions you used that created an unfavorable experience for them, and that you wish could have been prevented or avoided.
2. **Reparation** Seeking to understand your partner's perspective on how your words or actions made them feel, and then requesting to offer aid to support their healing process so the intimate relationship can be restored.
3. **Release** Liberating yourself from ruminating thoughts that produce future feelings of shame or guilt by consistently checking in with your partner to receive validation that you are providing the appropriate aid to supplement their healing process.
4. **Restraint** Practicing self-control by slowing down and processing the future outcomes your words and actions will have on your partner prior to selecting what you say or do.

Fear

We fear that the relationship will not last
We fear that our partner will escape our grasp
We fear that the road will be tough
We fear that we will not be enough
We fear that we may fall short

We fear that a marriage could end in court
We fear that there will be a breach in trust
We fear that our partner will cheat on us
We fear that there will be a loss of respect
We fear that there will be neglect
We fear that we will have to share
We fear that the issues may go beyond repair
We fear that we will get hurt
We fear that the relationship will not work
We fear that the relationship could last forever
We fear that we will remain together

I believe couples fear being together when they have not taken the time to define what togetherness looks like, because people fear what they cannot see. Partners who do not define what they need, want, and expect from their intimate relationship will fear the relationship itself. Fear is an internalized emotion that has its origins in our own thoughts, beliefs, and experiences. In order to prevent fear from blocking our ability to express care for our inti-mate partner, we first have to alter our current thoughts and beliefs by filtering them through new experiences. New experiences can include changes in our behaviors from one relationship to the next.

In working with intimate partners who have decided to dis-solve their relationship, they often state that their biggest regret is the time wasted due to the fact the relationship did not work. I hear these partners define the time together as a waste, and in doing so they forget about all the moments and memories they created while together. They also forget about the lessons they learned along the way. If we see our lives as one big timeline, then none of our experiences are wasted if we can use them to improve the future. This applies to intimate relationships, because we have the choice to reflect on the things we did not like from previous relationships and set boundaries against those things so that they won't be present in our future relationships. The four basic experiences that take place in our relationships that can produce fear are pain, rejection, disloyalty, and abandonment. Once partners learn how to assert themselves by setting boundaries in their relationships that limit or prevent these negative experiences from reoccurring, they will be able to remove fear and demonstrate care for each other.

Why Therapy Helps

To fear getting hurt by your intimate partner is equivalent to fearing living life itself. Despite how hard we try, it is impossible to avoid all pains, hardships, and struggles from occurring at some point in our lives and our relationships. Although it is impossible to evade relationship adversities, establishing expectations prior to expounding on relationship commitments can reduce the fear of future heart-ache. When we decide to form an intimate relationship with another imperfect human, we have to take the time to establish expectations. Therapy assists couples with developing rules that govern the relationship so that each partner can love fearlessly. Therapists help couples to develop relationship rules by helping each partner process what they want and don't want based on their family origins, past relationship histories, and future life goals.

During a premarital counseling session, I witnessed a female partner share how she wanted the same type of marriage her mother and father had. This was problematic for her partner to hear because he had a different expectation. The female partner described her parents as inseparable and her portrayal of their marriage included two people who chose to share every phase of their lives together, including work, hobbies, and socialization. As the female partner continued to illustrate her vision of marriage,

I witnessed her fiancé becoming more and more uncomfortable. After picking up on his nonverbal cues, I asked him to share with his partner what he was experiencing. His response was that he felt like their most pertinent relationship problem up to this point was that she wanted to spend too much time together. As we proceeded with therapy, it became clear that these two people had different expectations for their relationship. The male partner shared during multiple sessions that he was not ready to give up his space but feared losing his relationship. The female partner expressed how she disliked feeling as if she had to make her fiancé spend time with her, but also feared losing him. Despite both partners expressing their incompatibility for one another, their fears of being alone outweighed either of them choosing to end the relationship and find more compatible partners.

Therapy took a turn for the couple after they were given an assignment that involved writing a brief autobiography of how they saw their lives together after ten years of marriage. Each of their stories illustrated two miserable spouses who were involved in a marriage that eventually went crashing down in flames. The real aha moment came when I asked them both if their stories were based off on any actual marriages they witnessed, and they both said *yes*. The female partner shared that she thought of her partner's parents' marriage, because they ended up divorcing. The male partner said he too based his story off of his own parents' marriage, because his dad never wanted to spend a lot of time with his mom. As the couple concluded therapy, they were able to identify the fear of being together as greater than the fear of not being together. Therapy assists couples with identifying, processing, and treating their fears, so that they do not come to fruition.

The Four Basic Fear-Provoking Relationship Experiences

1. **Pain** Hurt or discomfort that is felt during a relationship when you are vulnerable with someone who does not reciprocate your expectations.
2. **Rejection** When an intimate partner communicates they no longer care for you based on how they treat you or how you failed to treat them.
3. **Disloyalty** Betrayal, unfaithfulness, or dishonesty inflicted by an intimate partner who you gave your trust to.
4. **Abandonment** The voluntary or involuntary departure of an intimate partner due to death, disconnection, or a loss of desire to stay in the relationship.

$\mathscr{Conclusion}$

THE FOUR TOOLS YOU WILL NEED TO BE SUCCESSFUL IN COUPLES COUNSELING

Value

It goes without saying that in order to get something of value, you have to pay a cost. Grant Cardone, who is a famous entre-preneur and author, constantly makes the point that "when value exceeds price, price is no longer the issue." This statement was true for a young couple I treated who sought out therapy to save their marriage after the male partner had an affair with a coworker while his wife was pregnant with their first child. I received the initial call from the female partner, who could barely keep her-self together as she explained her situation while crying profusely through the phone. At the time, I was still an associate level clini-cian practicing under supervision, and offered a below-market rate of eighty dollars for an hour-long couples therapy session. During the initial appointment, the couple stated they were homeless and did not have an address to put on file. I asked how they intended to pay for the sessions and she replied, "Salvaging this marriage means everything to me so we will find a way."

At the conclusion of the session the male partner handed me three wrinkled up twenty-dollar bills with oil stains on them. He explained that he had made the money working on cars. His wife covered the twenty-dollar difference by handing over fourteen one-dollar bills and a small sack of coins that equaled the final six dollars, which she made from tips at a local diner waiting tables. This couple came back every week and, over time, the coins turned into paper, the paper transitioned into a debit card, and the debit card turned into disbursements from a health savings account offered by an employer. They completed the initial treatment plan and gained healing from the husband's act of infidelity, but continued therapy to build a stronger foundation together as life partners. They both transformed themselves to gain higher levels of income and man-aged to purchase a home. This couple invested in therapy and, in return, they received new lives together—something so valuable that it far exceeds any price. These two special people taught me that when value exceeds price, price is no longer an issue. I am thankful to have witnessed this experience early in my career, because it rein-forced the value therapists provide to individuals, couples, and families. I refused to further reduce my fee and compromise the value I provided to those depending on me to deliver nothing less than my best effort every session. In the words of Grant Cardone, "If it is important to you, you will find a way."

Commitment

Time is the most valuable commodity we have, and where we spend it determines our commitments. I seek to serve couples that are committed to each other, because I want to help those who first desire to help themselves. This method also reduces therapist burnout and lessens the chances of compassion fatigue, which is a common disorder among healthcare professionals. From the beginning of the process, I inform clients that therapy will assist with changing bad relationship behaviors and will also help couples to plant new seeds of safety, communication, understanding, and feelings of care. However, if either partner chooses not to apply the information and skills learned in the sessions, they will not experience the results they are seeking. These couples still gain value from therapy because from this process they get to assess their individual and joint relationship commitment levels. But one of the risks of couples therapy is learning that you or your partner are no longer committed to performing the acts and doing the work that make relationships function. Committed couples plan out their schedules to accommodate routine sessions that are never canceled unless an emergency arises. These couples also complete the recommended assignments given by the therapist, seek to grow as individuals simultaneously, and give their therapist open and honest feedback along the process. When I sense that one or both partners may not be ready to complete all of these tasks, I politely inquire about their commitment levels. Just like an attorney who will not take a case to trial if they believe there is not a winning chance, I do not take on clients who I believe are uncommitted to the process. In doing so, I am communicating that my goal is to effectively treat the issues and concerns being brought into therapy, and I cannot do that with uncommitted partners.

Patience

Therapy should be approached like attempting to complete a marathon and not like running a sprint, because it takes time, patience, and endurance. More often than not, intimate partners who seek therapy are searching for relief, but therapy does not provide immediate long-lasting results overnight. Although my clients do feel support starting from the first session, it still takes time to achieve the long-term aid for which they are searching. Emotions take time to heal and routines take even longer to become habit-forming behaviors. It is unrealistic to use therapy as a quick fix, and if this is your intention then therapy will not work for you and your partner. Building a relationship designed to stand the test of a lifetime is like building a skyscraper. Tall buildings require deep holes dug during the onset so that their steel foundational beams can be anchored in strong bedrock. Treating lifelong relationships requires the therapist to dig deep into the couple's families of origin, behavioral patterns, and relationship needs before they can build the foundation that anchors both intimate partners together forever. Couples who want to achieve quicker results often do seek out individual therapy in conjunction to receiving couples therapy. I highly recommend this approach if one or both partners displays a history of untreated trauma, mental illness, or are experiencing forms of grief and bereavement. I personally practice exclusively as a couples therapist and will refer clients to seek individual therapy simultaneously to prevent an unequal balance of power that can threaten the therapeutic alliance. My process is not a requirement and most therapists will be willing to treat both partners independently.

Couples need to seek motivation from small victories in order to stay engaged during the treatment process. This can come from participating in the weekly assigned homework, sharing with your partner what they are doing correctly instead of always focusing on the aspects of the relationship that aren't working, and making the time to engage in activities that pump joy back into the relationship.

Hope

Hope is a combination of optimism, confidence, courage, anticipation, chance, expectation, and faith. Hope is a requirement for couples entering therapy. The bottom line is that couples have to be prepared to have hope that doing the hard work that is required to unlock the gifts of a blissful intimate relationship will work and is worth it.

I know all too well the stress and weight a relationship can put on you, but I promise that if you have selected the right per-son to invest time in, then all of the pressure you put on fixing the relationship can produce diamonds in the end. I learned this lesson firsthand after my wife (who, at the time, was just my girl-friend) became pregnant with our first child while we were in our second year of undergraduate studies attending different universities three hours apart. Getting pregnant instantly created an "us against the world" mentality and, in that moment, I took my first steps into manhood by choosing to put my relationship first. I had known other young men who had become teenage fathers. Many had said outright that they would to do whatever it took to be there for their child, but this didn't always include being present in the relationship with the child's mom. I made the choice to love my son by first learning how to love his mother. This included leading by example—we both worked hard on ourselves by completing our degrees on time and worked even harder on building our inti-mate relationship. My wife made me earn her hand in marriage by committing to her through my actions. While in college, I worked two jobs from Monday through Thursday and attended classes during the day. Thursday nights when I got off work, I drove three hours to spend the weekend with her and my son until Monday morning when I had to wake up at 5 a.m. and drive three hours back to my school for classes that began at 9 a.m. I did this routine for two and a half years with no complaints, but instead with the hope that my efforts would build a solid family foundation. I recall my internship preceptor telling the story about how he witnessed me at a restaurant he visited valeting cars and running back and forth with the passion that someone would only have if they were working for more than just tips. He was right—I was working to provide for my family. The focus and dedication I had for my wife and son was built on the hope that I would be a good husband and father. That hope can only be measured by my work. The same goes for couples seeking to build or rebuild their intimate relationships in therapy.

I hope what you've learned here will help you determine whether couples therapy is right for you and your partner, and will help to ease the transition into therapy.

About the Author

Chris A. Matthews is the founder and clinical director of Relationship Counseling Group, a private therapy practice based out of Charlotte, North Carolina that specializes in treating couples and families. Chris is a licensed marriage and family therapist (LMFT), licensed clinical addiction specialist, (LCAS), certified clinical supervisor (CCS), and approved supervisor for the American Association of Marriage and Family Therapy (AAMFT). Chris earned his bachelor of science in public health from the University of North Carolina at Charlotte (UNCC), and both a master of science degree in organizational leadership and a master of arts degree in marriage and family therapy from Pfeiffer University. For more than a decade, Chris has worked in a variety of mental health settings providing education and counseling to a diverse population of individuals, couples, and families.

In 2016, Chris made a choice to predominantly treat couples. Since that time, he has accumulated thousands of hours delivering counseling to intimate partners seeking healing from a variety of relationship issues. Through this journey, Chris used the experience and training he gained as a marriage and family therapist to author this book and help more couples determine if couples therapy is right for them.

In addition to Chris's formal training, he incorporates his life experiences as a husband and father of three into his practice of therapy. In 2006, Chris and his wife unexpectedly became pregnant with their first child while dating and attending college. Immediately following the realization that he was going to be a father, Chris chose to learn everything he could about starting a family. His journey led him to his pastor, who simply prayed and sent him on his way. Chris sought more guidance and was introduced to therapy by way of his university's counseling center. Chris's personal counseling journey provided him with the life direction he was seeking and, furthermore, gave way to his calling as a therapist. Chris shares this story with clients to assure them that they too can have both their faith and therapy.

To learn more about Chris A. Matthews, visit his personal website ChrisAMatthews.com. Visitors can send him messages directly, view material focused on strengthening their personal relationships, and request to hire Chris for speaking engagements, trainings, clinical supervision, and consultations.

Made in United States
North Haven, CT
10 March 2022

16967439R00124